How to
GET THINGS DONE

How to
GET
THINGS
DONE

Organize your life and achieve the results you want

Ann Jackman

THUNDER BAY
P · R · E · S · S

San Diego, California

Thunder Bay Press
An imprint of the Advantage Publishers Group
5880 Oberlin Drive, San Diego, CA 92121-4794
www.thunderbaybooks.com

All notations of errors or omissions should be addressed to Thunder
Bay Press, Editorial Department, at the above address. All other
correspondence (author inquiries, permissions) concerning the content
of this book should be addressed to Hamlyn, a division of Octopus
Publishing Group Ltd., 2–4 Heron Quays, London E14 4JP, United
Kingdom.

ISBN 1-59223-227-2
Library of Congress Cataloging-in-Publication Data available upon
request.

Printed and bound in China.

1 2 3 4 5   08 07 06 05 04

CONTENTS

Introduction

What motivates us to start up projects and make changes in our lives and work? Have you ever wanted to make changes or start projects but have failed to get them off the ground? Perhaps you have had a good idea and started planning how you were going to achieve it, but quickly lost interest after you considered more carefully how much work would be involved. Alternatively, you may feel that you have neither the skills nor the imagination to make the changes that you want to make.

Increasingly, many of us have less time to do the things we really want to do. We are driven by the fast pace of the world around us and the demands of others, both at work and in other areas of our lives. Yet we seem to want to achieve more. We are surrounded by images of people who have successful lives and beautiful homes. We are told that it is easier than ever to have it all. But how do we achieve this?

Many of us want to make changes in our lives and work. Some of us may want to make a career move, as we feel we have become stale in our current job. Others may want to build an extension to their home, creating additional living space. Whatever the project we have in mind, we need to be able to plan it and see it through to the end.

CASE STUDIES: BEN AND PAT

Here are two examples of changes that the people involved wanted to initiate.

For ten years Ben has planned his retirement in a rural area. He will achieve it next year by following a series of well-planned steps. Not everything has gone smoothly; for example, poor performance in the stock market made it necessary for him to make last-minute changes to his retirement plan and to adjust his goals for purchasing property in the area in which he wanted to live. However, because of his determination to see his plan through to the end, Ben has faced and overcome the barriers that threatened to sabotage his project.

Pat worked for fifteen years in a large public-sector company, where she was promoted to a senior management position. After her last promotion, she received training as an internal organizational development (OD) consultant, a role that she enjoyed and developed for three years. However, because of the company's career-development policy, her next position within the company would involve moving back into a senior management role. She did not want to do this because her interest in OD had developed and she wanted to continue working in this area.

Both these major changes would bring about improvements to their quality of life. Ben's change was internally motivated by a long-held dream of a life in his chosen location following early retirement. Pat's career move was precipitated by the inflexibility of a company to allow one of its senior managers to follow the career she wanted. While the career move was externally driven, Pat knew what she wanted to do and her motivation arose from her desire to continue working in her chosen field.

THE CHANGE EQUATION

Many projects that we initiate are linked to achieving improvements in different aspects of our lives and work. The only difference is the scale and scope of these changes. The "change equation" helps us to understand this more clearly:

Change = dissatisfaction + vision + first steps > cost involved

This equation demonstrates that change will not take place until all the components have been met. Therefore, we need to be dissatisfied with the current situation, have some idea of where we want to go, and identify some first steps toward achieving this goal; but we will not change until the sum of all these components is greater than the cost involved.

For Ben, one of the costs was financial—could he afford his new life? For Pat, the cost was leaving the security of an organization in which she had worked for some years and the people whose company she enjoyed.

CASE STUDY: JANE

The change equation applies to smaller projects, too.

Jane wanted to create more space in her home. It was a small house with two bedrooms and she had insufficient storage space for her clothes (dissatisfaction). She decided to convert the small bedroom, previously used for guests, into a dressing room (vision). This involved thinking imaginatively about how she might create extra storage space and still provide a place where guests could sleep.

She did some research and found a seat that could be converted into a bed and spoke to a carpenter about designs for built-in storage (first steps). The main cost was financial, so she planned the change when she knew she would have sufficient funds available and checked with her bank to make sure that converting the bedroom would not reduce the overall value of her property. Having satisfied all four components of the equation, Jane was ready to make the change.

REASONS FOR CHANGE

We make changes in our lives and work for all sorts of reasons. Some common motivators for change are:

boredom with the existing state of affairs

excitement about new opportunities that are there for the taking

loving change for its own sake

life transitions, such as middle age or retirement

external factors, such as children leaving home

economic factors, such as inheriting money or needing to economize

finding it difficult to develop, grow, or move forward within one's existing situation

unplanned events, such as divorce

HOW THIS BOOK WORKS

Having an idea and initiating change or implementing projects are two different things. Many of us have started projects, only to abandon them halfway through. There are many reasons for this, and these will be explored in this book. The good news is that barriers to change can be overcome, and we can follow a system that allows us to succeed in making the changes we want to make in our lives through the projects we undertake.

This book has been developed to help you see projects through from start to finish. Whether the project is big or small, this book provides you with a system that can be applied to any project, from decorating a room to changing your job.

Obviously, some projects take longer to implement than others, and some will have far-reaching effects. However, there are some key steps that you can take to maximize the success of any project, large or small. This book aims to introduce you to these steps and provide you with the motivation and confidence to succeed.

Section 1: Knowing Yourself

Helps you identify your strengths and weaknesses and develop some knowledge about your capabilities. It also helps you identify the key skills you will need to develop in order to succeed in seeing projects through to their completion.

Section 2: Key Skills for Achieving Success

Provides expert advice on maximizing your strengths and improving the areas of weakness identified in Section 1 through the implementation of ten key skills.

Section 3: Ten Stages to Success

Introduces you to a structured route, in ten stages, to completing projects satisfactorily, from identifying when you are ready for change to celebrating the successful implementation of the change.

Section 4: Practical Exercises

Provides you with some simple practical exercises to assess your understanding of the concepts presented in this book and to provide you with the confidence to get things done.

Section 1

Knowing Yourself

This section will help you analyze and identify your **strengths** and **weaknesses,** which can either help or hinder you in achieving what you want, and to establish your "Personal Portfolio." You will also learn, through a series of simple exercises, how to develop your knowledge about your own particular capabilities. The section goes on to help you identify the **key skills** you will need to develop in order to succeed in seeing projects through to their completion.

WHAT IS KEEPING YOU FROM ACHIEVING YOUR GOALS?

Having an idea and implementing it are two different things. All of us have strengths and weaknesses that can help us or hold us back in achieving our goals and plans. Some of us believe that we have no willpower and that we will never have the determination to achieve what we want. Others are frightened of failure or lack confidence. Here are some common barriers or pitfalls that can stand in the way of getting things done.

Waiting for something to happen

This can be a multitude of things, such as someone else taking the initiative or the responsibility, winning the lottery, or your partner leading the way. The reality is that the longer you wait, the less likely you are to get things done. Yet it is often tempting to put things off by leaving the responsibility to others. Taking responsibility is a key component of implementing projects successfully.

Not knowing what you want

From an early age, we are taught about other people and what they have achieved, as well as their ideas, aspirations, and challenges. We are rarely encouraged to think about our own achievements, strengths, and weaknesses. It can therefore be difficult sometimes to identify what you want and what your priorities are in your life.

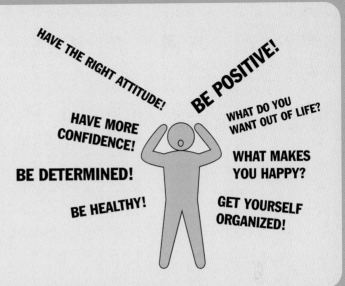

HAVE THE RIGHT ATTITUDE!

BE POSITIVE!

HAVE MORE CONFIDENCE!

WHAT DO YOU WANT OUT OF LIFE?

BE DETERMINED!

WHAT MAKES YOU HAPPY?

BE HEALTHY!

GET YOURSELF ORGANIZED!

Thinking you need to tackle the whole project all at once

Sometimes the sheer size of a project can be daunting and make the task seem just too difficult. Thinking of the project as a large task that cannot be broken down can sometimes keep us from getting started, and also makes it harder for us to sustain our motivation because it seems overwhelming. Organizational skills are essential for success.

Failing to set goals

Some of us like to live for today and have a built-in resistance to setting goals. Goal-setting is crucial to effective project implementation. Research shows that over 90 percent of people who set goals achieve them.

Fear of failure

Some of us develop a false belief that we should be always be perfect and that failure is a bad thing. In fact, most of us learn best from the things that go wrong in our lives. It is the failures that can teach us valuable lessons. Yet we continue to blame ourselves when things don't go well.

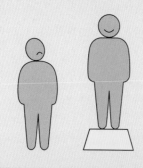

Comparing yourself with others

Many of us compare ourselves to others, having often been taught that others are smarter, better educated, more attractive, or nicer than us. This constant comparing can lower our sense of self-esteem and have a negative effect on our confidence. How many times have you said, "I would really like to do this, but I'm not good enough"?

Forgetting to involve and influence others in making and implementing our plans

Some projects, particularly the larger ones, require the assistance, support, and cooperation of others. It can be easy to overlook this and to forget to bring in "key stakeholders" (see page 52) at an early stage.

Failing to prioritize and manage our time

"Other things always seem to get in the way!" is a common excuse. It is critical that you prioritize your time to achieve your plans. Otherwise, life can intervene.

Not having the necessary skills

We often lack confidence because we don't think that we have the necessary skills to achieve our goals. Sometimes this is true; for example, we may lack assertiveness in particular areas of our lives. In many cases, however, we simply fail to recognize the valuable skills that we do have.

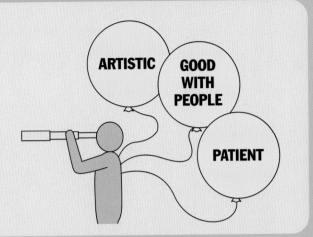

Lack of willpower

Having the courage and willpower to achieve what you want is not always easy, particularly when obstacles get in the way. Developing willpower is about maintaining self-discipline and handling the fears that are holding you back.

Any more?

You will surely be able to add to this list when thinking about your own experiences in getting things done.

The first step in succeeding in projects and making changes in our lives is to know ourselves, our strengths and weaknesses, our skills, and our patterns of behaving in different situations. This is a huge topic and it will take most of us a lifetime to get to know ourselves completely, but there are some key things that are important to know about yourself when implementing projects and making changes.

DEVELOPING
SELF-KNOWLEDGE

The exercises in Section 1 are designed to develop and build on your knowledge about yourself. Be as honest as you can. The exercises may seem a bit daunting at first, so just tackle them on your own time when you are ready. None of the answers are right or wrong, but are aimed at helping you identify how you prefer to behave and providing you with some insight into how these preferences might affect your motivation and determination to see changes and projects through to the end.

 It is a good idea to start up a "Personal Portfolio" of your strengths, weaknesses, skills, and reflections. Some people find it useful to use a loose-leaf binder to which new pages can be added and others can be removed when they are no longer relevant.

EXERCISE 1:
REFLECTION

This exercise can be very encouraging when you are thinking about embarking on a new project. It enables you to reflect on a previous successful project that you have completed and asks you to ponder some questions that will help you identify what you and others did to ensure the success of the project. The exercise can also help build your confidence by reminding you about the barriers you overcame in achieving your goals. Follow Steps 1 and 2 on page 19.

Some of us believe we have no willpower . . . others are frightened of failure or lack confidence.

STEP 1

Think about a project that you have been successful in implementing in the past. Write down the answers to the following questions:

- **What did you do to achieve the successful implementation of the project?**
- **How did you get started?**
- **What skills did you use?**
- **What help did you enlist?**
- **What barriers got in the way and how did you overcome them?**
- **What were the three main things that you did that you believe ensured the project's success?**
- **What were the main feelings you experienced during the project?**
- **What have you learned about your own strengths and weaknesses through undertaking this project?**
- **If you were to undertake a similar project in the future, what would you do differently?**

STEP 2

Ask some other people who were involved in the project to answer the same questions and give you some feedback about how they viewed your success. Compare these responses with your own and add to your list of strengths and weaknesses.

EXERCISE 2:
YOUR PERSONAL JOURNAL

 Linked to the reflection exercise above is another method that you can use to get to know yourself and your responses or reactions to successes and failures. This exercise involves keeping a Personal Journal as part of your Personal Portfolio.

It is not always easy to remember our successes—we tend to focus more on our failures. However, we can learn from both our successes and our failures. Use the following method to record significant successes and also events that may not have gone so well. Take a page and divide it into two halves as follows:

WHAT HAPPENED	MY BEHAVIOR
Note here what happened, what other people were involved, what they did, and what you think they were feeling and thinking.	Write down your thoughts and feelings about this event. What did you want to say and do? What did you actually say and do?

After the event, wait a few days and then read over your account of the event again. Looking at what happened, how do you feel about it now? What do you think about it? What have you learned from it? What are you going to do now or in the future?

We can learn from our failures.

EXERCISE 3:
KNOWING WHAT YOU WANT
AND GOAL-SETTING

Human beings tend to fall into two categories: those who think ahead and plan their futures and those who like to live their lives in a spontaneous way and live mainly for the moment. Both of these positions are valid; however, people who prefer to set goals and plan ahead tend to have more success in implementing projects. Look at the following statements and decide which ones apply to you. This will help you understand which category you fall into.

"Generally, I prefer to plan for tomorrow."

"I tend to live for today and don't think much about the future."

"I am clear about what is important for me to focus on in my life and work right now."

"I know what I would like to be doing in five years."

"I believe that having goals keeps me from being spontaneous."

"It is more important for others to have goals than for me to have them."

"I love change for its own sake."

"To be happy with change, I need to have a plan."

Different methods of goal-setting, to satisfy both personality types, are covered in Section 3 (see page 98). So, even if you prefer to live life for today, it is possible to set goals that meet your preferred ways of operating. Goals need not be restrictive; the secret is to set goals that allow you to be flexible and to make alterations to them if necessary.

WILLPOWER AND MOTIVATION

Willpower and motivation can, on occasion, elude even the most self-disciplined of people. It can be very easy to become distracted or find that, on certain days, you feel that you want to be doing anything but the tasks you know you should be doing.

Some of us have more staying power than others. Which of the following statements apply to you?

"I always do my work before I allow myself to play."

"I can play at any time."

"I tend to put off until tomorrow what I could do today."

"I love to see a job right through to the end."

"I hate to be disturbed when I have settled down to my work."

"I love interruptions, as they break up my day."

"I am easily distracted."

"I can't relax until I've completed my tasks for the day."

Those of us who are less likely to be distracted or finish our work before going out to play will generally have more "natural" willpower. However, all of us can learn to minimize distraction and develop willpower whatever our preferences may be.

Set goals that allow you to be flexible.

TAKING RESPONSIBILITY FOR YOUR LIFE AND WORK

It can be easy to put things off for all sorts of valid (and not so valid) reasons. The more you procrastinate during projects or when introducing changes, however, the more difficult both getting started and completing the project can become. The task then takes on enormous proportions.

How many times, when you finally get down to doing something that you have been putting off, do you say to yourself, "Well, that wasn't nearly as difficult as I thought it would be!"?

Don't just wait for something to happen.

These exercises can help you identify where you are procrastinating:

WHAT ARE YOU WAITING FOR?

List all the things that you are waiting for. Think of work and other areas of your life. The more areas you identify, the more likely you are to prefer that others take responsibility for those areas of your life and work. Notice any patterns that emerge during your thinking. For example, is there a common thread running through the things you are waiting for? This can help you identify areas that you may feel unsure about, lack confidence in, or simply don't want to tackle.

WHY ARE YOU WAITING?

Having identified your list and noticed any patterns, ask yourself if you really want to undertake this project, and if yes, why are you procrastinating? Do you need to enlist the help of others, develop some skills or confidence, or deal with your feelings of anxiety about the project or change? Being assertively powerful means taking the initiative. Instead of waiting for something to happen, you can take the first step.

Make some notes in your Personal Portfolio.

FEAR OF FAILURE

One of the main reasons for fear of failure is the belief that you need to get everything 100 percent right all of the time. Failure means that you are not achieving this state of perfection. The desire to be perfect is normally learned early in our lives. For example, if a child is told often enough by a parent or a teacher that scores of less than 100 percent on their examinations are not good enough, they can quickly develop perfectionist patterns and behaviors in several areas of their lives.

The reality is that perfection is impossible to achieve. We all make mistakes, and nobody can be right all of the time. However, many of us try for that elusive 100 percent when less would do. Perfectionist patterns can interfere with time management, self-management, and building effective relationships, and can also cause us high levels of stress.

ARE YOU A PERFECTIONIST?

Answer the questions below to identify any perfectionist tendencies you may have. Once again, there is no wrong answer; for example, setting high standards is a good thing, but being too hard on yourself when you fail to meet them can lower your self-esteem. The more questions to which you answered yes, the more likely you are to fear failure and be reluctant to take risks, such as when making changes.

Do you set high standards and then criticize yourself for failing to meet them?

Do you find it hard to make mistakes?

Do you find it hard to aim for less than 100 percent?

Are you hard on others who fail to meet your standards?

Is it important for you to be right?

HOW DO YOU COPE WITH FAILURE?

This exercise can help you cope with setbacks and failures. Answer the questions as honestly as you can and think about strategies that you might use to deal with failure in the future.

For each question, answer **often, sometimes,** or **never.**

SECTION A: **POSITIVE REACTIONS**

Do you: see **failure as an inevitable** part of a person's life?

try to **learn from your failures?**

make **contingency plans** in case you fail?

try to **understand why** the answer was no?

maintain good relationships with the people who made the decision, even if you disagree with it?

express your **disappointment** assertively?

use your network to find out why you lost?

maintain your allies so that you can win in the future?

withdraw so that you can **rethink** and try later?

face up to failure and try to turn it around into success in the future?

help others cope with their disappointment?

support the decision once it's been made?

explain to others why the decision was made?

maintain your **positive attitude** in the face of defeat?

If you answer "often" or "sometimes" to over half of the questions in section A, you are well on your way to maintaining your power and influence through the way you cope with failure.

If you answer "often" or "sometimes" to a high proportion of the questions in section B, you are in danger of letting your failures undermine your power by handling them badly.

SECTION B: **NEGATIVE REACTIONS**

Do you: **feel like a failure?**

take it personally?

feel inclined to **play it safe** and not risk failure in the future?

get very angry with the decision-makers (if the decision was not yours to make)?

burn your bridges?

continue arguing after a firm no?

push and **confront** so that people dig their heels in?

fail to support an unwanted decision when others make the decision?

HOW DID YOU SCORE?

If you got a high score on section A and a low score on section B, then you are letting your emotions interfere with your ability to be strategic. People do feel passionately about the projects they are involved with. It is therefore natural for them to lose their tempers and their objectivity when they suffer defeat. It is easy to feel rejected, threatened, or put down if you fail to get the answer you want. Yet, although passion and anger can be good, they can be destructive if they are not directed into productive channels. Take another look at the points in section A of the questionnaire and see if you can start to use some of these strategies the next time you lose a battle.

Record your insights and strategies in your Personal Portfolio.

IDENTIFYING YOUR SKILLS

A useful exercise is to think hard about what you do well, rather than always focusing on your failures and consequently undervaluing yourself. You may be surprised at what this reveals.

INVENTORY OF SKILLS AND POSITIVE QUALITIES

Draw up a list of all the things you are good at. Keep going until you have identified twenty or more skills, and then identify the same number of positive qualities that you possess.

Think about your skills in the broadest context. For example, if you are a parent who has chosen to stay at home to look after your children, you might not identify good time management and organizational ability as a particular skill, but rather as something you have to do to get things done. However, many people believe that these skills are very difficult to develop and they should therefore be valued.

So take the opportunity to do a bit of boasting. List your skills and qualities on a sheet of paper with the following headings and then add them to your Personal Portfolio. It can be useful to involve another person to prompt you and ask questions that will identify all of your valuable skills and qualities.

MY SKILLS—I AM GOOD AT:	MY POSITIVE QUALITIES—I AM:
1	1
2	2
3	3
4	4
5	5
6	6
7	7
8	8
9	9
10	10
11	11
12	12
13	13
14	14
15	15
16	16
17	17
18	18
19	19
20	20

ASSERTIVENESS AND INFLUENCING SKILLS

Assertiveness is the ability to determine and ask for what you want, set priorities in your life and work, and achieve your goals in a positive, direct way, without violating the needs and rights of others. It is crucial in helping you to initiate and negotiate within the projects and changes that you want to undertake.

Most of us can be assertive in situations where we feel confident, but find it difficult in others. For example, some people might find it very easy to be assertive in meetings at work, but find it harder to be assertive with friends who ask them to go out on evenings when they would rather stay at home. It is the normal human condition to be assertive in some situations and not in others.

Answer the following questions to help you to assess how assertive you think you are in each of the four different situations.

AT WORK

How do you respond when:

you have to confront a subordinate or coworker for continual lateness, sloppy work, or dishonesty?

nosy coworkers interfere in your private affairs?

you notice that someone has worked particularly well or made an extra effort?

you are given unjust criticism?

you are criticized legitimately by a superior?

you feel that your employer persistently demands a lot more of you than you are paid for?

you receive a compliment on your appearance, or when someone praises your work?

IN PUBLIC

How do you respond when:

you find yourself with an unhelpful store clerk?

you take back an item that has been broken or a garment that has shrunk?

the waiter in a restaurant deliberately ignores you?

the food that arrives on your plate is overcooked, cold, or bears little resemblance to what you ordered?

you have been waiting in a long line and someone barges in front of you?

the doctor dismisses you with a vague comment when you ask for more information?

someone lights up a cigar at the next table just as you are about to start eating?

a salesperson has gone to considerable trouble to show you some merchandise that is still not quite suitable for your needs?

you are sitting in a library and the person next to you starts talking on his cell phone?

you suspect you are being sold inferior goods?

AMONG FRIENDS

How do you respond when:

a friend persistently uses you as a shoulder to cry on?

a friend wants to borrow something that you need yourself?

others are putting down something you value highly?

a friend makes what you consider to be an unreasonable request?

someone is making nasty remarks about a person who is important to you?

you want to ask for the repayment of a loan?

you are upset by a racist or sexist comment?

you have to negotiate with a friend about which film to see or where to meet?

you feel put down or disregarded by a friend?

AT HOME

How do you respond when:

you want some privacy at home?

you want to say yes to an invitation, but your partner has other plans?

you want to say no to a proposed visit by a relative?

everyone leaves the dishes for you to clean?

you want to say no to a child's request?

one of your parents criticizes you?

Select an example from each of the above four categories that you think you handle less well than you would like to. Identify how you think you behave in these situations.

Ask yourself the following questions:

"What am I saying and doing in these situations?"

"How do I feel about my behavior in these situations?"

"What are my short-term gains or payoffs for behaving in this way?"

"How do I think my behavior is affecting the other person?"

"What are the long-term negative effects of this behavior on others and myself?"

Then select an example from each of the categories that you think you generally handle well.

Ask yourself these questions:

"What am I saying or doing that I am pleased about in dealing with these situations?"

"What are the risks involved in behaving in this way?"

"How do I think my behavior is affecting the other person?"

"What are the long-term benefits of this behavior on others and myself?"

After you have carried out the analysis, make some notes in your Personal Portfolio of what you have learned about your behavior in different situations. For example, are there any patterns emerging? Do you want to be more assertive? Do you overuse any types of behavior that serve you less well? The behaviors will be defined in more detail in Section 2.

Focus on what you do well.

PRIORITIZING AND MANAGING YOUR TIME

The ability to plan, organize, and manage time is a crucial element of project management and implementation. These skills can be learned, but many people find them difficult to do well. Our relationship with time will have a direct impact on how we manage our projects and changes.

Answer the series of questions below to help you to assess your time-management skills.

Do you: **tackle the most difficult tasks early in the morning?**

write a list of "things that must be done today"?

ever say no when asked to do something?

ever ask why when invited to go to a meeting?

think that other people waste less time than you do?

give priority to matters that are urgent, rather than to those that are important?

put all tasks into priority order and work on them in that order?

tackle one task at a time, finish it, and then move on to the next one?

accept all unscheduled interruptions?

prefer doing things yourself rather than give them to others to do?

ask other people how they organize their time?

NEXT STEPS

Now you are in a position of strength, having assessed your current skills, strengths, and weaknesses. Review your responses to the above questions and exercises and ask yourself, "What does this tell me about myself?"

Add your findings to your Personal Portfolio. Discuss these with some people who are close to you; for example, a coworker, friend, or family member. Encourage them to give you feedback and their personal observations.

It can be easy for us to focus on our weaknesses rather than our strengths. Remember that it is your strengths that will help you the most to succeed in the projects and changes that you want to achieve. So these are as important as your weaknesses.

Sections 2 and 3 of this book will help you build on your strengths, eliminate or improve your weaknesses, and develop your skills. Section 4 sets out some useful exercises to help you check your understanding and gain the confidence to apply your skills.

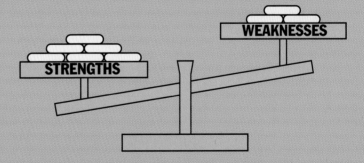

Your strengths will help you succeed.

Section 2

Key Skills for Achieving Success

Section 1 helped you assess your **strengths** and **skills** and identify areas you want to improve.

This section provides you with expert help in developing those weaknesses that you think might be holding you back from implementing the projects and changes that you would like to achieve.

Ten key skills are highlighted to form a **"Resource Pack"** that will help you make the changes you want. Some general exercises are included in this section to help you work through the theory in a practical way.

SKILL 1
HOW TO FIND MOTIVATION AND WILLPOWER

The first step to success is really to want the project to happen and to have sufficient motivational factors in place to make the effort worthwhile.

Case study

Gary wanted to give up smoking, and he had made several unsuccessful attempts in the past. He was asthmatic and knew that his smoking was damaging his health. He used to get bronchitis every winter. However, his enjoyment of smoking was greater than his motivation to stop.

Then two significant things changed. Gary met a woman who did not smoke and did not like to be around others who smoked. Gary's doctor, who was also a personal friend, told him that if he came into his office next winter with bronchitis, he would refuse to treat him!

These additional motivational factors were what Gary needed to provide him with some extra encouragement, and he succeeded in stopping smoking within six months.

The key to finding willpower is to want things to change. Without the desire, the willpower will be hard to find. By applying the change equation described in the Introduction (see page 8) to your situation or project, you can measure your will to change and the motivation to succeed. If the will is not there, then it is better not to undertake the project. This is not a sign of failure, but an indicator that it may not be the right time to make the change.

For some of us, finding additional motivational factors is not the cure for our lack of motivation or willpower. We can be really eager to make a change, but for some reason we just can't muster enough motivation to get started or we find ourselves losing enthusiasm as the project goes on. Improving courage and willpower is like developing muscles—the more you use them, the stronger they become. Then it can simply be a matter of practicing some simple exercises to help you develop your willpower so that you manage to sustain your interest and motivation.

Here are some exercises that can help you improve your willpower. They are divided into two categories: some that require an effort of will to do, and others where the act is quite easy but the will comes in trying to do them every day. Select the exercises that you think will work best for you.

The first step to success is really to want the project to happen.

EXERCISES THAT NEED EFFORT

When you are tempted to say something, **hold back and don't say it.**

When you want to do something immediately, don't.
Postpone it instead to a definite, specified time in the future.

When you want to postpone something, don't. **Do it right away.**

Do something that you know you don't want to do. This could be something simple, like walking to the store instead of driving.

Do something that you have never tried before, such as sampling a new type of dish that you think you won't like when you are in a restaurant.

Talk to a complete stranger each day.

Think of a situation that you would normally avoid, for example, making a complaint about poor service, and then do it.

EXERCISES THAT NEED REPETITION EACH DAY

Do these at the same time each day.

Go for a short walk.

Read a newspaper.

Sort through the mail.

Clean one of the rooms in the house.

Check your e-mail.

These exercises can be a great help in developing your ability to apply yourself to tasks that require self-discipline and courage.

SKILL 2
DEALING WITH YOUR NEGATIVE INNER VOICE

Another factor that can prevent us from finding the motivation to succeed in our projects is the negative inner voice that can suddenly leap into our thoughts. This voice normally appears when we are feeling vulnerable or when we are facing a particularly difficult challenge. The negative voice can be the result of beliefs we have come to accept about ourselves. We tend to be judged in society largely according to how we measure up to the relevant norms.

When compared to their peers, children may be exceptional at athletics, average at reading, or poor at mathematics. Adults constantly make comparisons about all aspects of the behavior of children—their intelligence, appearance, manners, work habits, ability to play with other children, and so on. In addition, adults often label children as, for example, loving or spiteful, friendly or mean, reasonable or selfish, cooperative or uncooperative, outgoing or shy. As we mature, these comparisons and labels are applied to all of us, first by adults, then by our peers, and eventually by ourselves.

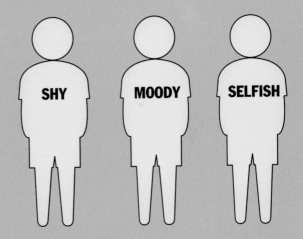

NEGATIVE COMPARISONS

Having internalized the standards and beliefs of those who judge us, we gradually come to describe ourselves in terms of how we deviate from the norm. For example, we may say to ourselves, "I may look pretty but I'm not clever." Listening to these negative messages can erode our confidence and lower our self-esteem.

Here are some more examples of negative and counterproductive talk that can speak to us.

Self-punishment: "What a stupid thing to do, you fool."

Negative self-labeling: "I'm mean, lazy, unattractive, etc."

Self-pressurizing: "I must," "I've got to," "I ought," "I should."

Making assumptions: "People won't like me if . . ."

Magnifying: "This is so difficult, I can't possibly handle it."

Catastrophizing: "If I don't ask the right questions, they won't be impressed and I won't get the job."

Believing there is no choice: "It's success or failure."

STOPPING THE INNER SABOTEUR

It is really useful to recognize these negative messages for what they are—inappropriate, irrational, and unreasonable. By becoming aware of them, you will begin to understand how you can block your own ability to succeed.

The next time you hear your negative inner voice, challenge it—is it really saying something valid and reasonable? Try replacing negative messages with positive, supportive ones. This process of challenge can provide you with a more accurate self-image and help raise your self-esteem.

"It's OK to make mistakes."

"I'm not stupid, although that was not the best decision I've ever made."

"I'm not lazy, just taking time to think about how to proceed."

DEVELOPING
SELF-ENHANCING THOUGHTS

Think for a moment and list three to five good things about yourself or your life—positive beliefs about your appearance, intelligence, range of interests, or life achievements (if necessary, return to the list of positive qualities you identified in Section 1 to help you). These should be truthful and concrete, such as "I have a nice smile" or "I am well informed about current affairs."

Now the goal is to increase how often you recall these self-enhancing thoughts. You can do this by following each positive statement with an immediate reward. Many every-day activities qualify as rewards—eating, drinking, playing a game, phoning a friend, and so on. Repeat a few of your self-enhancing statements just before the rewarding activity; in this way you reward yourself for thinking positive thoughts and these thoughts are strengthened by the pleasurable act that follows.

Carry your list of positive messages with you wherever you go. Take them out and read them when you are feeling down or lacking in confidence.

Achievements and
Positive Qualities

"I am friendly."

"I am intelligent."

"I am healthy."

TAKING RISKS

At any time during your project, you may be faced with making a decision or undertaking a task that feels risky. You may, for example, need to ask your boss for a big favor or make a decision that you know will displease a friend. Taking risks is an important part of making changes and implementing projects. To take risks, however, we need to confront our fears.

STEPPING OUT OF THE COMFORT ZONE

Our comfort zone is the area of our lives and work within which we can operate with comfort on a day-to-day basis. We feel that we are in control and can handle with ease any situation that comes our way. Working within our personal comfort zone enables us to operate with confidence and maximizes our likelihood of success.

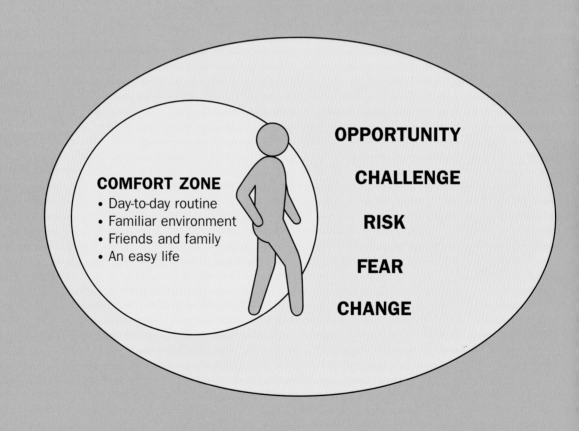

COMFORT ZONE
- Day-to-day routine
- Familiar environment
- Friends and family
- An easy life

OPPORTUNITY

CHALLENGE

RISK

FEAR

CHANGE

However, certain situations arise that can threaten to take us outside our comfort zone, such as a new or challenging opportunity. Our natural reaction is often to retreat into our comfort zone and bury our head in the sand in the vain hope that the situation will somehow disappear. We know that if we are to deal with the situation, this will mean taking a risk, with all of the associated fears inherent in that risk.

Our negative inner voice begins to take over and we start to catastrophize about what will happen if we step outside our comfort zone. Yet, to develop and move forward, to achieve change, and to be successful, we know deep down that we need to stretch the boundaries of our comfort zone outward, otherwise it will start shrinking in on us.

How many times have you felt fearful about something, and when you have plucked up the courage to confront it, the fear recedes and the situation seems less of a problem than you thought? Research has shown that approximately four out of five of our fears never materialize. Of the ones that do materialize, however, we often find that we can handle them anyway, because we are much more resilient and resourceful than we give ourselves credit for.

Therefore, when you are making changes or undertaking projects, it is useful to notice the types of fears you are experiencing that might keep you from taking the risks that you know you need to take if the change is going to happen.

This is not about being reckless, but about analyzing your fears and challenging the negative inner voice that might be preventing you from moving forward. Then it is about trusting your good judgment and repeating to yourself your internal mantra: "Just do it."

Four out of five fears never materialize.

Case study

As mentioned on page 7, Ben was planning for his retirement. While doing this, he experienced lots of fears, including:

having insufficient money to live on

leaving his friends and family behind

alienating his wife, who initially did not want to uproot and leave the city

being bored without his day-to-day routine of commuting to the office

discovering he had made a mistake in moving

failing to achieve his dream

He managed his fears by examining them and building strategies into his project plan to minimize and neutralize them, such as adjusting his financial plans when the stock market was giving him lower returns on his investments. By taking charge of his fears, he felt more in control of them and better able to move forward.

MANAGING YOUR FEARS

It is not always possible to reduce all your fears. It is all right, however, to feel fear, since at the other end of the scale lies excitement. Excitement is a positive feeling and an essential one to experience when making changes. Here are some strategies for managing your fears so that they don't get in the way of your success.

Strategies

- Talk about your fears to friends and family; seek and listen to their encouragement.
- Practice taking small risks first, and notice the feelings of satisfaction and achievement associated with them.
- Gradually increase the level of risks you take.
- Use affirmations to challenge your negative inner voice; for example, by repeating to yourself how well you are performing a particular task if your fear is that you will fail in achieving it.
- Allow yourself to feel fear; it is a valuable indicator that you are on the brink of a change. But then try instead to get in touch with the excitement that the change will bring when you have achieved it.

Handling your fear is an essential skill to draw upon when you are undertaking change. Many of us fear change, and if we allow our fear to control us, we can lose sight of the reasons why we have decided to make the change in the first place. It is not always easy for us to handle our fear, and our first instinct is often to run away from it. Remember, however, that you don't have to deal with your fear on your own, and that if you do confront your fears, they will often disappear.

We need to stretch the boundaries of our comfort zone.

SKILL 3
ASSERTIVENESS FOR INFLUENCE

There are many situations where assertiveness can help you to succeed with your projects and changes. Here the focus is on two key areas:

1. Taking the initiative, remaining positive, and setting goals
2. Identifying and influencing your "stakeholders"

TAKING THE INITIATIVE, REMAINING POSITIVE, AND SETTING GOALS

Assertiveness is one of the behaviors that we can choose to use when dealing with other people. It is also a state of mind that reflects our attitudes, beliefs, values, and self-esteem.

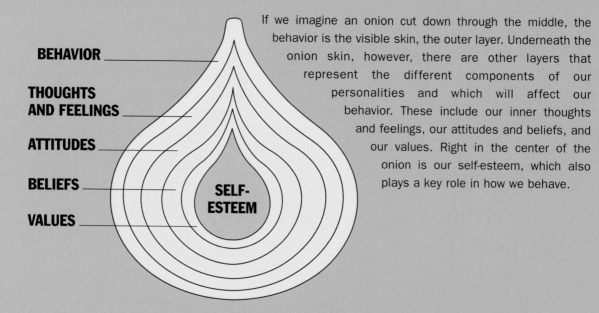

BEHAVIOR

THOUGHTS AND FEELINGS

ATTITUDES

BELIEFS

VALUES

SELF-ESTEEM

If we imagine an onion cut down through the middle, the behavior is the visible skin, the outer layer. Underneath the onion skin, however, there are other layers that represent the different components of our personalities and which will affect our behavior. These include our inner thoughts and feelings, our attitudes and beliefs, and our values. Right in the center of the onion is our self-esteem, which also plays a key role in how we behave.

STEPS TO ASSERTIVENESS

By being: **a) clear about what she wanted,**

b) feeling positive about her intentions, and

c) taking the initiative,

Pat achieved a significant first step in moving toward her new career as a freelance consultant. She also practiced what she wanted to say so that she was in the best position to influence the other person, a more senior figure in her organization.

This was not an easy step for Pat to take, however, and she had to be careful not to revert to her preferred behavior in this situation— passive behavior—which would have kept her from achieving what she wanted.

Being assertive means planning and preparing what you want to say. It can seem time-consuming, but, as you can see from Pat's example, it can also reap rewards.

Take control and reap the rewards.

IDENTIFYING AND INFLUENCING YOUR "STAKEHOLDERS"

With larger projects, such as moving into a new house or restructuring a department, some people will have a key role to play and may present a barrier to the successful completion of the project. It is important to identify all the key people, or "stakeholders," who you will need to influence if the project is going to be successful. Stakeholders can be people who will be directly involved in your project, such as your family, or simply people you need to influence to make it happen. The diagram below illustrates some of the stakeholders involved in a plan to move into a new house.

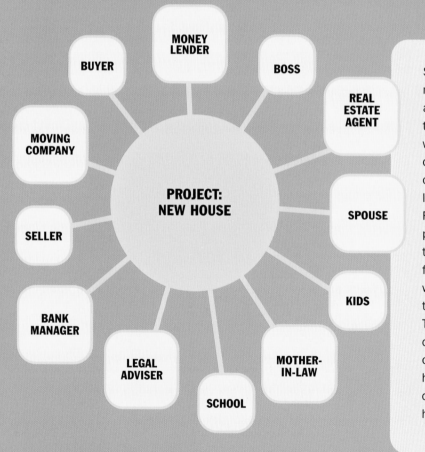

MONEY LENDER

BUYER

BOSS

REAL ESTATE AGENT

MOVING COMPANY

PROJECT: NEW HOUSE

SPOUSE

SELLER

KIDS

BANK MANAGER

LEGAL ADVISER

MOTHER-IN-LAW

SCHOOL

Sarah was planning to move into a new house and identified some of the stakeholders she would need to influence during the process. Some of the stakeholders are less obvious than others. For example, Sarah had to persuade her mother-in-law that a move farther away from where she lived would not be detrimental to their relationship. There were also financial considerations, and in order to afford her ideal house, she would need to convince her boss to give her a raise.

PREPARING TO MEET THE BOSS

After you have identified your stakeholders, you will need to influence them. Some will be quite straightforward, but others may be more of an unknown quantity. For example, in the stakeholder diagram, it is likely that Sarah will have a good idea of her husband's view of the planned move. However, she may not be so sure of her boss's response to a request for a raise. It would therefore be useful to do some research before she meets her boss so that she is fully prepared and can be assertive and confident.

THE MEETING MODEL

Many people will find the following model useful. Ask yourself these questions before meeting with any of your stakeholders.

What power do you have to influence the other person?

What is your objective?

YOURSELF	*What are your strengths and weaknesses?* *What power do you have to influence the other person?* *How do you feel about your relationship with the other person?* *How might you prepare for the meeting?*
STAKEHOLDERS	*What are their strengths and weaknesses?* *What might their position be?* *How much power do they have to grant your request?* *How do they view your relationship with them?*
THE TASK	*What is your objective?* *Where might you compromise?* *What is your ideal outcome?* *What might you expect realistically and what is your bottom line or fallback position?* *What resources might you need?* *What are the constraints?*
THE ENVIRONMENT	*Where is the best place to hold a meeting with the person you want to influence?* *What sort of atmosphere do you want to create—formal or informal?* *When would be the best time to have a meeting?* *Will you be free from interruptions?*

Assertive behavior will normally bring you the most effective results in influencing others, because it is the behavior that it is most useful to apply when you want to develop and sustain relationships.

Case study

Let's take Jane's room change (see page 9). One of the people she needed to influence was her husband, Richard. He thought that changing the bedroom to a dressing room would be counterproductive and would reduce the value of the property. He could also see no point in employing a carpenter, as he could build the new closets himself.

Richard's position posed two main problems for Jane that she needed to address and overcome.

- **How could she convince Richard that converting the bedroom was a good idea?**

- **How could she convince Richard to employ a carpenter (she had witnessed Richard's attempts at carpentry before)?**

Jane did her homework and spoke to the bank about the possibility of the change reducing the value of the property. The bank confirmed that the room change was more likely to add value to the property, as it provided more storage and you could still fit a single bed into the room. She presented the figures to Richard and proposed that they go ahead with the change as planned. Richard agreed. The second scenario was not so easy. Richard found it hard to understand why Jane wanted to employ a carpenter when he could just as easily do the job.

FIVE ASSERTIVE SKILLS

These can be used in a variety of situations and provide a structure within which to work. They are not presented in any particular order, but it is worth spending time figuring out specifically what you want to say, as this is often enough to influence the other person.

1. Being specific

This involves deciding what it is you want or feel and being prepared to say so specifically and directly. It involves keeping your statement simple and brief. For example, the most direct way to refuse a request is to say no. However, we often use other options, which are at best watered down and at worst confusing.

2. Repetition

Sometimes referred to as the "broken record technique," this skill helps you to stay with your statement or request by using a calm repetition. Using this technique, you can maintain a steady position without falling prey to manipulative comments, irrelevant logic, or argumentative bait designed to take you away from your point.

3. Dealing with manipulation

This is also known as the "fogging technique" or "fielding the response." In order to communicate most effectively when others are trying to manipulate you, indicate that you have heard what the other person said, but without getting baited by what they say and straying away from your point. This skill allows you to acknowledge the other person's response and still continue confidently with your statement or request, instead of feeling defensive or aggressive.

4. Workable compromise

It is important to remember that when there is a conflict between your needs and wishes and those of someone else, assertiveness is not about winning at the expense of the other person. So you need to negotiate from an equal position. This means finding a true compromise that takes both parties' needs into consideration.

Compromising on a solution to a difficult situation need not jeopardize your self-respect. In any situation where you are preparing to be assertive, it is useful to identify what your ideal outcome would be, what your realistic position might be, and what constitutes your fallback position or bottom line.

5. Self-disclosure

This skill allows you to disclose your feelings with a simple statement such as "I feel nervous" or "I feel guilty." The immediate effect is to reduce your anxiety or guilt, thus enabling you to relax and take charge of yourself and your feelings.

Jane used these five assertive skills to help her in the dialogue that took place between her and Richard.

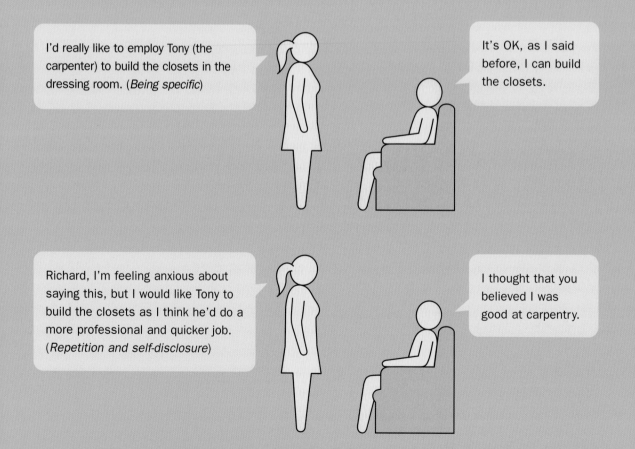

I'd really like to employ Tony (the carpenter) to build the closets in the dressing room. (*Being specific*)

It's OK, as I said before, I can build the closets.

Richard, I'm feeling anxious about saying this, but I would like Tony to build the closets as I think he'd do a more professional and quicker job. (*Repetition and self-disclosure*)

I thought that you believed I was good at carpentry.

I do think that you are great at some projects, but I don't think carpentry is one of your strong points and I think we should ask Tony to build the closets. (*Fielding the response*) How about we compromise and Tony builds them and you paint them? (*Workable compromise*)

Well, if you really don't think I could do them properly . . .

It's not that I think you couldn't do them properly, it's just that Tony is a skilled carpenter who has been trained to build closets (*Fielding the response*) and that he will produce excellent results in a shorter time.

Oh, all right then, but let's see if we can get him to reduce his price a bit.

All five assertive skills were used in the dialogue between Richard and Jane. By remaining calm, clear, and honest, Jane was able to influence Richard to employ Tony. Jane also chose the right time to approach Richard; she raised the subject when they had the time to discuss it.

Being assertive is not always easy, and it can take a lot of time and energy. However, it is the only behavior that will build your self-esteem and provide you with the best opportunity to influence others successfully. Therefore, in the long term, the extra effort required will usually be worth it.

Assertiveness is about compromise and negotiating a win-win outcome.

SKILL 4
HANDLING CONFLICT

The dialogue between Jane and Richard (see pages 56–57) presented several opportunities for conflict to arise. The definition of conflict in this situation was when there was a difference in position, or point of view, between two parties that could not be resolved. It was through using assertive behavior, which enabled Jane to remain calm and in control, that she was able to avoid conflict.

However, the dialogue could have gone very differently had Jane used different behaviors.

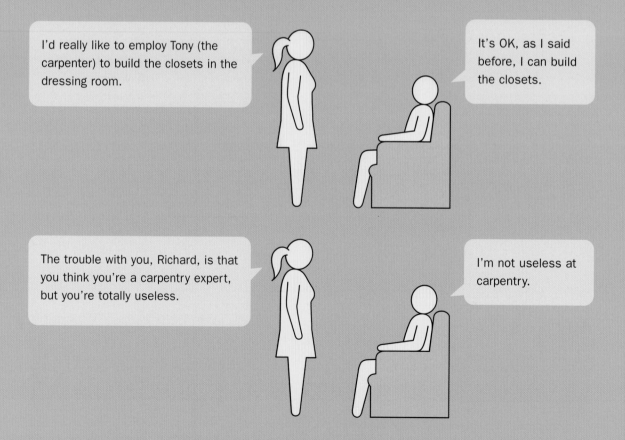

I'd really like to employ Tony (the carpenter) to build the closets in the dressing room.

It's OK, as I said before, I can build the closets.

The trouble with you, Richard, is that you think you're a carpentry expert, but you're totally useless.

I'm not useless at carpentry.

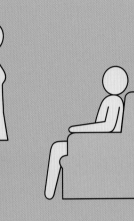

Many of us will be familiar with such aggressive dialogue. A probable outcome is that the issue will remain unresolved, with the likelihood that Richard will go ahead and build the closets—without Jane's agreement—while they become further entrenched in their positions, both thinking they are right.

RESOLVING CONFLICT

Conflict situations are those in which the concerns of two parties appear to be incompatible. In such situations, a person's behavior falls into two basic categories: **confrontation** (the extent to which the individual attempts to satisfy their own concerns) and **cooperation** (the extent to which the individual attempts to satisfy the other person's concerns).

1. COMPETING
2. ACCOMMODATING
3. AVOIDING
4. COLLABORATING
5. COMPROMISING

Five approaches to resolving conflicts have been identified; all these approaches are useful and can be employed in different situations when conflicts arise. The skill is being able to select the correct approach for resolving each particular conflict. The two types of behavior described above can be used to define these five specific methods of dealing with conflicts.

1. Competing

This approach is confrontational and uncooperative. It is where an individual pursues his own concerns at the expense of the other person's. This is a power-oriented style in which someone uses whatever power seems appropriate—his ability to argue, his rank, his economic status—to gain the upper hand. Competing might mean standing up for your rights, defending a position that you believe is correct, or simply trying to win.

2. Accommodating

This approach is nonconfrontational and cooperative—the opposite of competing. When accommodating, an individual neglects his own concerns to satisfy the concerns of others; there is an element of self-sacrifice in this style. Accommodating might take the form of selfless generosity of charity, obeying another person's order when you would prefer not to, or yielding to another's point of view.

3. Avoiding

This approach is nonconfrontational and uncooperative. The individual does not immediately pursue his own concerns or those of the other person. This approach does not address the conflict. Avoiding might take the form of diplomatically sidestepping an issue, postponing an issue until a better time, or simply withdrawing from a threatening situation.

4. Collaborating

This approach is both confrontational and cooperative—the opposite of avoiding. Collaborating involves an attempt to work with the other person to find some solution that fully satisfies the concerns of both parties. It means digging into an issue to identify the underlying concerns of the two individuals and finding a solution that meets both sets of concerns. Collaborating between two parties might take the form of exploring a disagreement to learn from each other's insights, agreeing to resolve some condition that would otherwise have them competing for resources, or confronting and trying to find a creative solution to an interpersonal problem.

5. Compromising

This approach is intermediate in both confrontation and cooperation. The objective is to find some expedient, mutually acceptable solution that partially satisfies both parties. It falls on a middle ground between competing and accommodating. Compromising gives up more than competing but less than accommodating. Likewise, it addresses an issue more directly than avoiding, but doesn't explore it in as much depth as collaborating. Compromising might mean splitting the difference, exchanging concessions, or seeking a middle ground.

SELECTING THE APPROPRIATE
WAY TO HANDLE CONFLICT

The different approaches to resolving conflicts might be applied in the following situations.

COMPETING

When **quick, decisive action** is vital, e.g., emergencies.

On important issues when **unpopular courses of action need implementing**, e.g., cost-cutting, enforcing unpopular rules, and discipline.

On issues vital to company welfare **when you know you are right.**

To **protect yourself** against people who take advantage of noncompetitive behavior.

ACCOMMODATING

When **you realize that you are wrong**—to allow a better position to be heard, to learn from others, and to show that you are reasonable.

When **the issue is much more important to the other person than to yourself**—to satisfy the needs of others, and as a goodwill gesture to help maintain a cooperative relationship.

To **build up social credits** for later issues that are important to you (give and take).

When continued competing would only **damage your cause,** where you are outmatched and losing.

When **preserving harmony and avoiding disruption** are especially important.

To **aid in the managerial development** of others by letting them experiment and learn from their own mistakes.

AVOIDING

When **an issue is trivial,** of only passing importance, or when other, more important issues are pressing.

When you perceive **no chance of satisfying your concerns,** e.g., when you have low power or you are frustrated by something that would be very difficult to change (national policies, someone's personality, organizational structure, etc.).

When the potential **damage of confronting a conflict** outweighs the benefits of its resolution.

To **let people cool down**—to reduce tensions to a productive level and to regain perspective and composure.

When **gathering more information** outweighs the advantages of an immediate decision.

When **others can resolve the conflict** more effectively.

When **the issue seems tangential** or symptomatic of another, more basic issue.

COLLABORATING

To **find an integrative solution** when both sets of concerns are too important to be compromised.

When your objective is to learn, e.g., **testing your own assumptions** or understanding the views of others.

To **merge insights from other people** with different perspectives on a problem.

To gain commitment by **incorporating others' concerns** into a consensual decision.

Teamwork without hard feelings that have been interfering with an interpersonal relationship.

COMPROMISING	When **goals are moderately important,** but not worth the effort or potential disruption of more confrontational styles.
	When two opponents with equal power are strongly committed to **mutually exclusive goals,** e.g., in employee–management negotiations.
	To achieve **temporary settlements** to complex issues.
	To arrive at **expedient solutions** under time pressure.
	As a backup style when **collaborating or competing fails** to be successful.

EXERCISE IN CONFLICT ASSESSMENT

You can identify the appropriate style to apply to a real-life conflict, based on two key considerations:

- **the importance of the outcome**
- **the importance of the relationship with the other person involved in the conflict**

Below are ten pairs of statements. Each pair describes a conflict situation. In each case, circle the letter of the one statement that you think fits your conflict situation better.

P   *I don't really care what the other person thinks of me when the conflict is over.*
R   *It is important I have a good relationship with the person once the conflict is over.*

M   *It won't be the end of the world if I don't resolve this conflict.*
O   *I have vital interests at stake in resolving this conflict.*

P   *I don't have a significant personal or business relationship with the other person.*
R   *My relationship with the other person is important for business or personal reasons.*

M *The time and trouble needed to resolve this conflict might not be worth it in this case.*

O *I expect the resolution of this conflict to be worth my while if it goes reasonably well.*

P *In my relationship with the other person, there is very little sharing of feelings and information.*

R *My relationship with the other person is based on shared feelings and information.*

M *I don't expect resolving this conflict to affect future dealings with the other person.*

O *I won't be surprised if resolving this conflict sets the pattern for many future conflicts.*

P *My communication with the other person has been limited.*

R *My communication with the other person has been extensive.*

M *I will not feel any worse about myself if I end up thinking I lost the conflict.*

O *I won't feel really good unless I do well in this conflict.*

P *I am not dependent on the other person.*

R *We have common interests because of the ways in which we are thrown together.*

M *The issues at stake here are clear and straightforward.*

O *I suspect there are important hidden factors at stake in this conflict.*

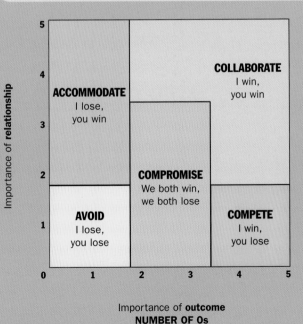

Scoring

Count your letter scores.

How many Rs did you circle?

How many Os did you circle?

Your responses can now be plotted on the model below to assist you in identifying the strategy that might be the most useful for you in resolving the conflict.

SKILL 5
CONFRONTATION

One way of getting the other person to move when all else fails is to use confrontation. This, when skillfully used, is a very powerful method of handling conflict, but it should only be used sparingly. People who are seen as very confrontational tend to be feared and avoided.

WHAT IS CONFRONTATION?

Confrontation is making explicit the difference between:

- **what you value and what the other person values.**
- **what you think and what the other person thinks.**
- **what you feel and what the other person feels.**

When you do this, you risk hurting the other person's feelings.

Confrontation also makes differences explicit between:

- **what you want to do and what the other person wants to do.**
- **what you actually do and what the other person actually does.**

When you do this, somebody has to change their behavior; the risk is that it may be you.

Conflict is inevitable.

Confrontation also makes differences explicit between what the other person says and what they do. When you do this, you risk making the other person angry or defensive.

HOW TO CONFRONT

1. Acknowledge the other person's position as legitimate.
2. Differentiate the other person's position from yours.
3. Check to see whether you have heard the other person clearly and that he has heard you.
4. Accept angry, hostile feelings in yourself and in the other person as real. Be responsible for your own feelings. Leave the other person free to feel differently.
5. Don't try to solve the problem until differences have been fully explained.
6. Ask the other person to describe his preferred solution. Be prepared to state (and differentiate) yours.

USING CONFRONTATIONAL STATEMENTS CONSTRUCTIVELY

The following statements are confrontational, but not aggressive, meaning that they can be used in a constructive manner to try to resolve conflict situations.

SKILL 6
MANAGING ANGER AND FRUSTRATION ASSERTIVELY

Conflict situations often cause us to feel angry or frustrated. If we allow our feelings of anger or frustration to build up, we can lose control of a situation and find it difficult to remain assertive. Below are some strategies for effectively handling and channeling your anger when conflicts arise.

RECOGNIZE

The first step in managing your anger and frustration is to recognize it. Learn to identify the signals that you are angry. For example, what are the physical symptoms that you display when you become angry? How do you behave? It can also be useful to notice the ways you have of denying your anger.

DECIDE

Then decide what to do with it. Mark it "for attention" and take time to look at it, either immediately or later. Generally, it is not productive to express your anger to another person until you feel in control of your emotions. If you think you need more time to calm down, take yourself away from the situation until you have regained your composure. The "avoiding" approach to handling conflict can be a very useful strategy here.

USE

Employ your anger as an energy source, using it constructively to power ideas and projects and to make changes.

EXPRESS

Give your anger a *safe* form of physical expression (later and/or in private, as appropriate). Strategies might include physical exercise such as swimming, running, and dancing, or shouting, thumping a pillow, tearing (unwanted) papers, or even tackling that household chore you have been putting off.

VOICE

Use the assertive skill of self-disclosure to voice your anger. Be sure to "own" your anger. Avoid saying "you make me angry." Just say, simply, "I'm angry." Be honest when you voice your anger and be careful not to downgrade it by, for example, saying, "I'm a bit annoyed," when in fact you are feeling furious. Also try to avoid modifying it by describing your anger as another feeling, such as "I'm upset" or "I'm unhappy." Treat your anger seriously, not lightly.

KNOW

Get to know your anger. Learn about it in all its shades and degrees of intensity. Discover its range—for example, from mild irritation to raging fury. It can be helpful to catch it in its milder forms and voice it then, rather than letting it develop any further. Your anger is a life-saving signal, so respect it and make friends with it. It is important when dealing with conflicts to separate present anger from past anger. In some situations and with some people, we can develop what is called "backlog anger." This is where anger builds up because we deny it or fail to deal with it. Avoid raking up old anger from the past. This will fuel the conflict rather than defuse or resolve it.

CONFRONT

Confront the situation using some of the techniques described in Skill 5 (see page 66).

RELEASE

Finally, let go of the destructive ways in which you abuse your anger, yourself, and other people—for example, by punishing or blaming yourself and others. Allow yourself to forgive and to let go.

SKILL 7
PRIORITIZING YOUR TIME AND MANAGING YOURSELF

The ability to manage yourself and set priorities when undertaking projects is crucial. Many of us set off with good intentions, but leave too little time to complete what we need to do, become distracted, or find that we are disorganized in our approach.

The main reference point for implementing our projects and change successfully is to have clear goals to work toward and to keep us focused (setting goals is explored in detail in Section 3). Skill 7 looks at how to ensure you work efficiently. In order to improve our use of time, it is important to understand where time goes. Our use of time can be categorized into two areas:

1. TIME SPENT ON USEFUL WORK   **2. TIME WASTED**

Time spent on useful work needs to be maximized, while time wasted needs to be cut to a minimum. Five strategies for making the most efficient use of your time are highlighted below.

1. THE IMPORTANCE OF PLANNING

Managing time more effectively means planning time—both yours and others'. Almost any task (writing, using the telephone, decorating a room, going on vacation) will be executed more effectively if a little time is given to planning it in advance. A sound plan of action, and the effective implementation of that plan, is the bridge across which an idea travels from the brain to the end result. Planning also allows you to handle several things within a project or change, and ensures that you give proper attention to each.

2. GOOD PLANNING

Once you have set your overall goals or objectives for your project or change, one of the most vital ingredients of planning is breaking a whole job down into parts and deciding the relative importance of each. Follow these five simple rules:

1. Gain firm **knowledge** of your project or change.

2. Leave a **margin for error**—don't plan on tight deadlines.

3. Know your **resources**—human and material.

4. Plan **flexibility** so that you can make minor amendments where necessary.

5. Plan with **care**. Be proactive rather than reactive.

Scheduling

To consolidate your time, schedule sensible blocks into your plan according to the nature of the task. For example, longer blocks will be necessary for writing the first draft of a book, and fewer, shorter ones for redrafting or amending the text. If feasible, try scheduling certain tasks on particular days of the week, and set aside parts of other days for working on major tasks.

Alternatively, schedule different activities into the day according to your own best working pattern. It makes sense to work on the most important part of your project when your energy levels are at their highest—your "prime time."

Know how long you can concentrate on one thing at a time—this varies from person to person. Remember that working with other people demands longer blocks of time.

Plan your time carefully.

3. USING A DIARY

A diary is an invaluable tool when planning any project or change, whether large or small. Adopting the following procedure will both help you in the planning stages and act as a reminder as the weeks and months progress.

PLAN YOUR YEAR

Write all the following items in your diary at the beginning of the year:

- **One-time events**
- **Vacations**
- **Family get-togethers**
- **Priority tasks or projects**

PLAN YOUR MONTH

At the start of each month, plan your diary as follows.

- **Take stock of free days and identify what you want to use them for.**
- **Don't cancel days allocated to your priority tasks or projects.**
- **Make a point of attending important events.**
- **Reserve time for short-term important tasks.**

PLAN YOUR WEEK

Adopt effective weekly planning habits.

- **Have clear tasks/objectives for the week.**
- **Schedule time for activities.**

PLAN YOUR DAY

Adopt effective daily time-management habits.

- **Create a daily plan first thing in the morning before you do anything else.**
- **Plan to do the hardest and most important things first.**
- **Review your daily tasks/objectives for five minutes at the end of the day and readjust your plan for the next day if necessary.**

Following the planning steps outlined above can make a significant difference to the effectiveness of your project-management skills. It has been proven over and over again that an hour of planning saves much more time when the project is carried out.

4. EFFECTIVE TIME MANAGEMENT

Having planned your project or change, it is important to manage your time effectively on a day-to-day basis. One way to approach this is to **eliminate** unnecessary tasks, **insulate** your schedule to allow you to use your blocked-out time for your projects, and build in sufficient factors to your project to give you time to **concentrate**.

Elimination

This involves, among other things, making sure you are not blindly following existing habits and practices. Eliminating could include:

- **Simplifying work practices:** For example, do you need a specialist to undertake specific parts of your project (such as Jane, see pages 54–59, in her desire to employ a carpenter to build the closets in her newly designed room)?
- **Better communication:** Assertiveness can, as we have seen, defuse or avert conflicts and ensure that you make it clear to others what you want.
- **Delegating to others:** You don't have to do it on your own; who else can help you free up your time so that you can undertake your projects?
- **Avoiding procrastination:** This can be done by developing courage and willpower.

Insulation

It can be helpful to think of your time in two parts: uncontrollable time and controllable time. **Uncontrollable time** includes time spent on things such as responding to others' demands and requests, phone calls, meetings, visitors, and chatting. **Controllable time** is time that is self-imposed and discretionary, and can be spent however you like.

Insulation means giving yourself an uninterrupted block of controllable time so that you can use it effectively. Ideally, the block of time should coincide with your own prime time, the time when your mental faculties are at their peak. It is then a good idea to group the uncontrollable time into similar task areas and put them together into specific time slots within the day. For example, setting aside half an hour at the beginning and end of the day to read and respond to

It has been proven over and over again that an hour of planning saves much more time in execution.

e-mails. Make your plan very clear and have a "quiet time" that others are aware of, thereby increasing their cooperation.

Concentration

Concentrating means undertaking your important activities during your controllable time. Then you will be working most productively and avoid spending too much of your time on unimportant tasks or trivia during the most important parts of your day or week.

- It is often helpful to use lists to remind you what needs to be done. Check off the items on your list as you achieve them in order to keep you motivated. Be realistic about the size of your list. Only draw up achievable lists, or they can have a demotivating effect when you fail to meet your daily objectives and tasks.
- Break down complex tasks into doable steps. Tackle each step, then give yourself a break. Don't try to concentrate for too long at a time.
- Be realistic—schedule only 50 percent of your time, as the rest will undoubtedly be needed for uncontrollable events.
- Prioritize your tasks on a day-to-day basis, using your project goals and objectives as a guideline. Divide all your tasks into the following categories and undertake them in priority order. Use the prioritizing system with your lists:

PRIORITY 1	*Important and urgent (tasks to be undertaken immediately).*
PRIORITY 2	*Important but not urgent (tasks that can be planned in at a future time).*
PRIORITY 3	*Urgent but not important (tasks that can be allocated to someone else or delegated).*
PRIORITY 4	*Routine (tasks that need to be undertaken at some time but can be deferred or delegated).*

5. TOP TIME-SAVING TIPS

Outlined below are some time-saving tips to help you manage your projects and changes well. Identify those you already practice and a couple of others you would like to try out.

DOING LESS

Delegate.

Say no.

Don't take work home from the office.

Discourage unnecessary meetings.

Don't attend to issues other people can do better.

Don't take on other people's problems when they should handle them themselves.

Don't get bogged down with details.

WORKING FASTER AND REDUCING DOWNTIME

Make deadlines and stick to them. Note them on a calendar.

Tackle a task the first time the opportunity arises—don't put it off.

Tackle important matters when you are more alert— it saves time and you will make a wiser choice.

Keep communications concise.

When dealing with someone you think may waste time on a decision or implementation, set a target date (or, better still, get him to set one).

Start and end meetings on time.

Use the telephone when it can save time.

WORKING MORE EFFECTIVELY

Plan your work and work your plan.

Establish your objectives clearly.

Make "to do" lists daily and weekly.

Set priorities.

Be realistic.

Be patient.

Plan all written communication.

Plan long phone calls.

Plan meetings.

Stick to agendas.

Keep a neat work area.

Take breaks during the day—a rest period revives you.

**Allow enough time for what you are doing—
rushing can cause more work in the long run.**

Don't assume that everything that was important yesterday is important today.

Build "thinking time" into your day.

Use your diary more fully—plan the day and set times.

Tackle jobs within your attention span.

Each day, finish what you start.

Schedule sensible time blocks.

Work on the most important part of your project when your energy levels are at their highest.

SKILL 8
EFFECTIVE DELEGATION

Most people know the basic principle of delegation, but the failure to convert this knowledge into practice can result in a busy person becoming overloaded. Knowing what to delegate and to whom when making changes and implementing projects can reduce your stress levels and ensure that you maximize the use of your controllable time by eliminating time spent on things that others could do.

Peter: design report ✓
John: research ✓
Gail: calculate figures ✓
Chris: book meetings ✓

PRINCIPLES OF DELEGATION

Whether you are delegating at work or at home, the same general principles apply. The aim of delegation is to get others to do the work and make the decisions that they can handle as well as, or better than, you can. You can't do it all—you are only one person and no matter how able, skilled, and energetic you are, there are limits to what you can accomplish. When you delegate, you become, in effect, many people, and you enlarge the scope of your achievement.

The main issue in delegation concerns deciding which tasks and responsibilities to retain and which to give to others. It therefore involves the following:

Planning: Thinking about to whom you want to delegate, what you can delegate in its entirety, and what others can help you with.
Decision-making: Consciously deciding which responsibilities you want to keep for yourself and which you can share with others.
Organization: Drawing up a plan of action and schedule for the task.
Coordination: Making sure that you keep an overview of the tasks you have delegated and ensuring that deadlines are met.
Reviewing: Checking on progress, adjusting deadlines, and reallocating tasks where necessary.

It is important to establish the limits of authority. When you delegate a task, also delegate the responsibility for doing it properly and the authority for getting it done. The other person should understand the importance of the task, the span of time he has to complete it, and the degree of authority. For example, can he make a final decision or can he only recommend? It is also important to agree on what sort of follow-up or review is necessary, and exactly what to expect. This is particularly important when the delegation is also a training or development exercise for the individual concerned. You therefore need to:

Define aims: Set objectives for the task.

Set standards: make clear the level of performance you require and set standards and boundaries around the task.

Coach the person to whom you have delegated the task: He may not get it right first time and will probably need your support at some stage during the delegation process.

Establish deadlines: Make them realistic, achievable, flexible, and coordinate them with other tasks within the project.

Measure progress: Set up regular review meetings or discussions and keep a note of important milestones.

WHAT SHOULD BE DELEGATED?

- Minor routine matters or matters that are urgent but not important
- Tasks that assist in testing people's abilities, as well as giving them experience
- Tasks that the person can do as well as, or better than, the person delegating the task
- Jobs requiring the specialized skills of another person; for example, Tony, the carpenter in Jane's decorating project (see page 54)

WHAT SHOULD *NOT* BE DELEGATED?

- All the work a person has to do
- Emergency tasks requiring your own skill, knowledge, and experience
- Jobs requiring unofficial action
- Matters that are an exception to policy or routine
- Matters that might have serious repercussions
- Work that is aimed at punishing or rewarding people

The model outlined below can help you further with selecting what to delegate and to whom.

**WHAT AM I
GOING TO DELEGATE?**

**SKILLS
REQUIRED**

TASK

**TO WHOM SHOULD
I DELEGATE?**

TIME SCALE

*You can't do it all—
you are only one person.*

FAILING TO DELEGATE

We all have different reasons for not wanting to delegate our projects and tasks to others. However, within any project or change, there is always room to delegate some responsibilities to another person. Here are some common reasons for failure to delegate.

Feeling indispensable—"If I don't do it, no one else can or will."

Lack of confidence in others

"I enjoy doing it myself."

Lacking delegation skills

Misguided benevolence and fear of overloading the other person

Fear of being accused of dumping unwanted tasks on others

Fear of loss of authority and need for control

Fear of inability to answer queries

If you can get over the barrier of asking others for help, especially when you are overloaded or know that others have as much or more expertise in particular aspects of the project, delegation can reap huge rewards.

GUIDELINES FOR DELEGATION

Follow these guidelines to ensure that you delegate well.

Ensure that the person concerned understands the extent of the delegation— set clear terms of reference, including levels of responsibility and authority.

Agree on a schedule for the task.

Build in regular reviews.

Tolerate mistakes—they are inevitable.

Praise and encourage the person to whom you have delegated the task.

Celebrate the successful completion of tasks.

SKILL 9
HANDLING STRESS

Stress is our body's way of letting us know that the demands that are being placed upon us exceed our ability to cope. We all need a certain level of stress to survive as human beings. The physiological changes that take place in our body when it prepares to deal with a stressful situation, such as making a presentation in public or attending an interview, equip us to deal well and competently in these situations. Then, when the stressful situation passes, we return to a normal state.

Problems arise, however, when we experience stress over an extended period of time and our bodies are maintained at an unacceptable level of readiness. This state of being can, in both the short and longer term, create negative symptoms that we need to watch out for and deal with.

Making changes and embarking upon projects can be stressful. It is useful to get to know our stress and how to deal with it if we are to be successful in implementing the changes that we want to introduce in our lives and work.

You need stress in your life!

SYMPTOMS OF STRESS

These vary from person to person, but they can be divided into four main categories:

1. Physical symptoms, including palpitations, nausea, muscle cramps, aches and pains, colds and other infections, fatigue, and indigestion

2. Emotional symptoms, including mood swings, irritability, feeling tense, anxiety, withdrawal, and feelings of powerlessness

3. Behavioral symptoms, including being prone to accidents, poor job performance, overeating or loss of appetite, lack of concentration, negativity, feeling drained

4. Mental symptoms, including indecision, memory failure, worrying, confusion, loss of sensitivity toward others, short-term thinking, loss of perspective

An important step to managing stress effectively is to get to know your stress in all its many forms and learn to recognize when you are experiencing stress at an early stage.

CAUSES OF STRESS

Stress comes from four sources, known as "stressors."

1. Situational stressors come from our situation, our environment, and our contemporary culture. They include unknown and unexpected situations, change, noise, depressing news, poor housing, being confined in a vehicle, and heavy workloads.

2. Major life events are events that have a significant impact on us in terms of how we live our lives and on our emotions. They include marriage, divorce, death, birth of a child, moving into a new house, poor health, and financial concerns.

3. Stressors caused by other people can be hard to handle. They include unreasonable demands or expectations, a bad atmosphere at work or home, and feeling misunderstood.

4. Stressors from within ourselves can be the biggest cause of stress. They include seeking perfection, expectations of self, the need for purpose and success, feelings of inadequacy, the need to be in control, and the need to be accepted and loved.

Learning more about the factors that cause you stress is a useful way of anticipating when you are likely to experience it. A single stressor is unlikely to create problems. Usually you experience a series of stressful events within a short period and it is the cumulative effect of these events that causes the stress symptoms to emerge.

DEALING ASSERTIVELY WITH STRESS

Learning to handle stress in an assertive way can be an invaluable tool in interrupting the stress pattern and reducing your stress to manageable levels. Stress can be debilitating if you allow it to continue without acknowledging and dealing with it. However, with a little practice, you can get to know your stress and welcome it as a life-saving tool. The following strategies should be helpful.

Become knowledgeable about stress

Ask yourself the following questions in relation to a stressful situation that you have experienced or are currently experiencing, or that has become a repeating pattern.

"What causes this stress?"

"When does it happen?"

"Where does it happen?"

"How does it affect me?"

"Do I affect anyone else?"

"Why do I react this way?"

"What can I do to reduce my level of stress in this situation?"

"Who can I ask to support me?"

Come to terms with your feelings

Acknowledge your feelings and share them with others. Emotions are a valuable indicator that things are either going well or not so well in our everyday lives. Try not to deny your feelings, but rather, accept them as valuable friends.

Develop effective behavioral skills

Ask for your needs to be met, avoid blaming others for situations, use your free time productively, learn to say no and yes for yourself, acknowledge problems as soon as they appear, take the initiative, and develop your sense of personal power.

Establish and maintain a strong support network

Don't be afraid to ask for direct help, rid yourself of destructive or nonsupportive relationships, and tell the members of your support network that you value their friendship.

Develop a lifestyle that will strengthen you against stress

Build in a little exercise each day, find time for relaxation, plan your use of time both in the long and short term, eat a healthy diet, don't smoke, and consume alcohol and caffeine in moderation.

Look after your mental health

Think positively, handle your negative inner voice, know your personal limits, do things you enjoy, and spend time on hobbies and special projects.

HOW DO YOU HANDLE STRESS?

Answer the following questions to check how you handle stress right now.

1. What factors are present in your life and work at the moment that are causing you stress?

2. How do these stressors affect you:

   - physically?
   - emotionally?
   - mentally?
   - behaviorally?

3. Do you typically respond to stress by:

   - acknowledging and dealing with it?
   - denying it?
   - ignoring it?

4. What might you do to manage your stress levels better in the future?

TURNING STRESS TO YOUR ADVANTAGE

You can use stress positively by keeping it within manageable levels and channeling the stress that fuels your energy sources into the projects and changes that you want to make. One of the key things that you can do to achieve this during your projects and changes is to focus on those areas over which you have control.

During projects, many of us spend a lot of time worrying about things over which we have little or no control. We waste a lot of time and energy in doing this. We can also waste time by failing to take action in relation to certain aspects of our projects that we can control, and procrastinate instead.

Both of these strategies cause us to experience frustration and stress from within ourselves. The diagram below illustrates this:

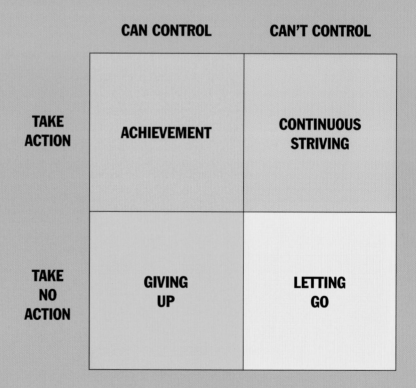

	CAN CONTROL	**CAN'T CONTROL**
TAKE ACTION	**ACHIEVEMENT**	**CONTINUOUS STRIVING**
TAKE NO ACTION	**GIVING UP**	**LETTING GO**

Learn to recognize when you are experiencing stress.

Case study

Ben spent a lot of time worrying about the decline of the returns on his investments, and his levels of stress increased each time he read a newspaper or heard a financial report on the television news. Eventually, he realized that he was worrying about something over which he had no control; he could not influence how the financial markets performed. His continuous striving was wasting energy and increasing his anxiety and fear. It was threatening to sabotage his goal.

So he decided to separate out the aspect of his finances over which he had control, namely how he responded to the economic downturn. By focusing on the area over which he had control, he was able to take action by seeking professional advice and adjusting his plan accordingly.

His anxiety levels dropped immediately, since he had taken action over something he could control and had also let go of worrying about things over which he had no control.

TAKING CONTROL

Try this out for yourself. Think of a situation that currently causes you stress and answer the following questions:

- Which of those factors that cause you stress have you little or no control over?
- Which factors do you have control over?
- How could you let go of worrying about those factors over which you have little or no control?
- What steps might you take to deal with those factors over which you have control?

By dealing with situations in this way, you can take control and move things forward without worrying unnecessarily. Ask a friend for help if you need to—remember, you don't have to do this all on your own.

SKILL 10
MAINTAINING HIGH SELF-ESTEEM

In order to achieve success in getting our projects started and being able to see them through to the end, we need to be able to handle the knocks, setbacks, and rejections that will inevitably occur. This is not always easy, as it means keeping our self-esteem at a consistently high level so that we can develop resilience and maintain the belief that we will succeed despite the barriers that might present themselves. Self-esteem is essential to our well-being and it is something that can be grown or allowed to diminish.

WHAT IS SELF-ESTEEM?

Although self-esteem has been discussed already in this book, it might be useful to spend a little more time defining the term and identifying strategies to maintain it at a high level. Self-esteem can be divided into two types.

FIRST TYPE

Internal sense of self-worth This is the ability to like and accept yourself with all your strengths and weaknesses. Having high self-esteem is not about being perfect; it is about accepting yourself as equal to others while recognizing that you are different and unique. It also includes accepting others in the same way, rather than as superior or inferior to you.

SECOND TYPE

External sense of self-worth This is the self-esteem that is reflected by other people. We get it from the positive or negative comments of others and our need for approval and acceptance. They do this in many ways, such as wanting to spend time with us, giving us praise, or seeking our advice. Other external sources of our self-esteem are the media, work, and relationships.

Most people rely heavily on external sources of self-esteem. This is a risky strategy, since it means that we might not get what we want from others, or conflicting messages cause it to be inconsistent, resulting in our self-esteem going up and down from day to day. For example, we might receive praise from our boss for working long hours on a project to get it finished and at the same time be criticized by our partner for never being at home.

DEVELOPING INTERNAL SELF-ESTEEM

The secret of maintaining high self-esteem is to develop the sources of internal self-esteem that will build a solid foundation that is difficult to knock down. Then, when the inevitable knocks and setbacks arise during our projects, we can quickly bounce back without our self-esteem being diminished. It is like comparing self-esteem to a tree:

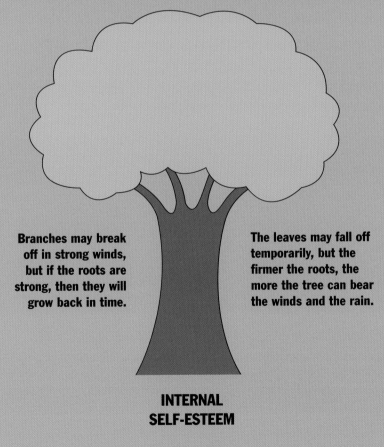

Branches may break off in strong winds, but if the roots are strong, then they will grow back in time.

The leaves may fall off temporarily, but the firmer the roots, the more the tree can bear the winds and the rain.

INTERNAL SELF-ESTEEM

The key skills and strategies that you need to adopt when undertaking projects are all covered in this book. Applying these skills and strategies will assist you in successfully developing your internal sources of self-esteem.

Building self-esteem in the long term can be achieved by:

taking the initiative

developing motivation and willpower

practicing assertive behavior

challenging your negative inner voice

setting goals

putting yourself first

taking physical and emotional care of yourself

taking risks

giving quality time to yourself

being aware of your self-growth and development

In addition, ask yourself the following questions:

How much of what I do is based on a need for reflected approval?

Whose eyes reflect back my measure of acceptability?

What standards do I have to measure up to?

Whose standards do I need to reach in order to qualify for acceptance within each category of my life—at work, at home, and in relationships with others?

It is only by developing self-acceptance that we can build up our self-esteem. To do this, ask yourself these questions:

Whose opinion really matters to me?

With those people, is there a conflict between what I do to please them and what I really want to do?

Remember that it is all right if we are making a choice to please these other people.

Self-esteem is essential to our well-being.

Section 3 continues to build on the skills described in Section 2, but focuses on the mechanics of identifying projects, setting and reviewing goals, and monitoring and celebrating success.

Section 3

Ten Stages to Success

Section 1 helped you identify your **strengths** and **weaknesses**.
Section 2 outlined some of the **skills** and **strategies** you will need
to develop to ensure success with your projects and changes.

This section follows a structured route to starting up and completing
projects satisfactorily, from identifying priorities for change to
implementation and review. You should use your Personal Journal
to make notes where appropriate.

STAGE 1
IDENTIFYING AREAS OF DISSATISFACTION

The Introduction presented the change equation (see page 8) and showed how you can use it to help you know when you are ready for change. It can be helpful to consider the different aspects of your life and work and use the equation to identify the areas or relationships that you are currently dissatisfied with.

Having identified your key areas of dissatisfaction, and because people often want to make several changes in their lives and work at the same time, in Stage 1 you will identify your priorities for change. This will also help you set in place some desired outcomes or visions for the changes and projects that you want to make. The method used here is called **domain mapping**.

DRAWING UP A DOMAIN MAP

A domain map consists of a series of concentric circles, broken up into segments like a dartboard, with you at the center. Each segment constitutes a "domain." Imagine you are standing on the summit of a mountain, looking down on the domains that represent the areas in your life that are causing you concern and with which you have some form of relationship (this can be a person or an aspect of your life). The domain map is completed in several stages.

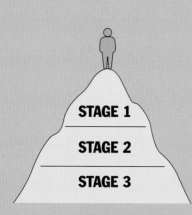

Stage 1 In the first circle away from the center, write in each segment an area of your life that you are dissatisfied with.

Stage 2 Write in the corresponding segment of the next circle, for each domain, a description of the present situation.

Stage 3 Go out to the next circle and describe how you would like that situation to be.

Case study

In the Introduction (see page 7), Pat was considering a career change because she had come to a point where she would not be able to use all of the skills she had acquired as an internal consultant within her organization. Looking at Pat's situation is helpful when illustrating how to draw up a domain map. At Stage 1, Pat allocated one segment to her career. In addition, however, there were other areas in Pat's life that she was dissatisfied with.

- She had no balance in her life; it consisted of all work and no play. She had no time for herself and she was unable to find time to exercise.
- She had a difficult relationship with her brother, which she wanted to improve.
- She wanted to create more space in her house and was considering having an extension built.
- She found it difficult to be assertive at work with certain key people and in certain situations.

Each of these above areas was represented within a separate segment or domain. You can see from the diagram on the right how Pat completed the first three stages of her domain map, using the "assertive behavior at work" domain as an example. This gave her a bird's-eye view of the aspects of her life that she was currently dissatisfied with, and also some idea of how she wanted things to be, following any changes she made.

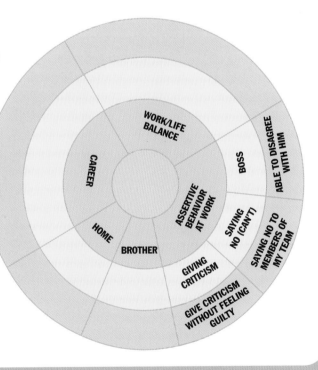

There will be more about the domain map later in this section. First, you need to see how you can use the steps undertaken so far to identify priorities for change and to clarify your intentions.

STAGE 2
IDENTIFYING PRIORITIES FOR CHANGE

In determining your priorities for change, you will need to identify which of the desired outcomes, set out in the third circle of the domain map, you want to begin working on first. How you choose your priorities will depend on your own sense of what your priorities might be.

MAKING DECISIONS

Here are some possible criteria to help you to decide.

Importance: This is the most important because it will bring about the biggest payoff for yourself and others.

Urgency: The effects of not getting it done will be the most serious.

Quickest benefit: It will show some results very soon.

Hardest to deal with: This is the most difficult, so you want to do it first in order to get it completed and out of the way.

Key to some of the other domains: It needs to be done first, because until this change is made, you can't move forward on the others.

Will: How much do you really want things to change?

Set your priorities and make things change.

Case study

Using the criteria opposite, Pat set her priorities for change in the following order.

PRIORITY 1	***Become more assertive with key people at work.*** *This was necessary in negotiating a career move and to help her to determine exactly what she wanted. This was also an area where Pat felt that she would see beneficial results in a short span of time.*
PRIORITY 2	***Make a career change.*** *This was a key area for change, as it affected other changes she wanted to make. She also had a huge amount of will to make this change.*
PRIORITY 3	***Build in time for herself.*** *This was an important priority because Pat would need time to think and plan her career change. She would also have to look after her physical and emotional well-being in making such a big career change.*
PRIORITY 4	***Establish a better relationship with her brother.*** *Although it was important to do this at some time in the future, there were other, more urgent priorities in Pat's life.*
PRIORITY 5	***Make a change in her living situation.*** *This was the least important priority, and although it would have been desirable to do it, Pat decided that she did not want to spend the money at this time. In addition, if her career move was to become self-employed, she might need to rethink her living space to fit in a home office.*

Priority 1 became Pat's immediate focus of attention. It was not such a major and important change as Pat's career move, but it had high priority because it equipped her with one of the key skills required to get her second priority started. Read about what Pat did to address this area of dissatisfaction in her life in Section 2 (see page 50). This illustrates that the project Pat identified, namely to "become more assertive with key people at work," was relatively easy to implement. She was clear about what she needed to achieve, and because of her training, found it easy to identify a plan of action and set goals. She identified the support she needed, then practiced her new skills in influencing the HR director. An assertiveness course helped her develop her skills further.

STAGE 3
SETTING GOALS AND ACHIEVING THEM

Only about 5 percent of people set goals, and yet over 90 percent of those who do set goals achieve them. Setting goals is an excellent way to raise the probability of success in implementing your projects and changes.

Why do so few people set goals? Some of the reasons were explored in Section 1 (see page 14). Remember there are those of us who prefer to plan for tomorrow and those who prefer to live for today. Other reasons for not setting goals are:

We don't know how to: We lack a method or formula for setting goals.
We don't have the time: We don't set aside time because we are too busy.
Fear of failure: If we don't have goals, we won't fail.
We can't see the point: "How will goals help me achieve what I want to?"
We don't see the need: "They're unnecessary, I'll just get on with it."

This stage shows you how to set goals with the minimum of effort and the maximum probability of success.

How can we attain those big dreams?

TRADITIONAL GOAL-SETTING

The traditional way of setting goals is to use a formula that is very precise and produces goals that are:
Specific, **M**easurable, **A**ctionable, **R**ealistic, and **T**ime-oriented.

SMART objectives are effective when used within organizations and business environments where goals need to be measured precisely and achieved within a set time frame; for example, the goals that are set for performance reviews. There is, however, an alternative approach that is more flexible and more suitable for the types of projects and changes that you will be embarking upon.

AN ALTERNATIVE APPROACH TO GOAL-SETTING

This approach is based less on facts and figures, but requires you to trust in the goal-setting process and to assume that you will succeed. It also requires you to think big and to expect the best. Here are some guidelines:

Set your goals as large as possible—think big. This will create excitement, the desire to achieve your goals, and a sense of challenge.

Be specific in describing your goals—a clear and specific statement can be helpful in keeping you focused. Writing your goals in the present tense, as if you have already achieved them, can be a very powerful tool. This helps to create the belief that you can achieve your goals.

Write your goals down and tell others about them. It is also a good idea to include pictures, objects, and other representational items to describe them.

Use both logic and creativity in developing your goals; for example, use visualization exercises to help you.

List the blocks and barriers between you and your goals and formulate a plan to overcome them.

Break down the tasks involved into daily units.

Discipline yourself to take the necessary steps to achieve your goals—develop your willpower.

Don't worry too much about how to achieve your goals—having some clear first steps worked out is often a more effective approach than a detailed plan of action.

Be flexible, review your goals from time to time, and adjust them where necessary—for example, if you need more time to undertake certain tasks.

Assume success rather than failure and try not to concern yourself with whether you can or cannot achieve your goals. Learn to trust that the process will deliver them. This creates an expectation that the goals will be achieved.

Take responsibility for the outcome—positive or negative.

Reward yourself when you achieve your goals.

Think big and expect the best.

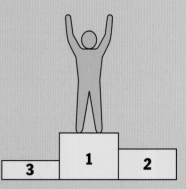

Case study

Future mapping

Recall that Ben was planning a move to another part of the country for his retirement (see page 7). He set the following goal and wrote it in the present tense as if he had already achieved it. This process is called "future mapping."

It is July 2004 and I am now living in a new house in the countryside with my wife, Ellie, and our dog, Barney. The house has been built to my specifications and I have sufficient funds in the bank and a good pension to enable me to retire from my job in the city.

Ben set his goal five years earlier; however, by writing it down as if he had already achieved it, he felt motivated and driven toward achieving his goal.

Achieving your goal

Ben succeeded in achieving his goal by implementing the ten key guidelines detailed below.

1. Thinking big

Ben was not originally going to build his own home, but he had been looking for a house for some time and had found nothing suitable. He therefore developed an ambitious plan to have a house built to his specifications.

2. Writing it down

He wrote down his goal, but he also gathered together lots of pictures of the type of house he wanted and put these in a folder with pictures of his wife and their dog. He also had some pictures of the area that he wanted to live in.

3. Involving others

He involved his family and friends in his dream so that it became more real and enabled them to share in his goal.

4. Visualizing

He used visualization techniques to create in his mind a picture of the perfect house and a sense of how the house would look when it had been decorated.

5. Planning

Ben planned his goal well; he developed annual, monthly, weekly, and daily planning systems. This enabled him to break his plan down into smaller tasks that did not daunt him. He avoided the fine detail in the planning process, but set some key milestones and first steps to achieve.

6. Overcoming barriers

There were lots of barriers threatening to keep Ben from achieving his goal. There was the problem of the stock market downturn, which reduced his pension (see pages 7 and 87). He had to adjust his thinking about the type of house he wanted and made alterations to the size of the property to cut down on costs. He dealt with each barrier as it arose and developed strategies to remove them.

7. Reviewing

He also reviewed his goal regularly to check that he was still on course and to adjust schedules. This was particularly important during the building of his house when bad weather or shortage of labor delayed completion.

8. Thinking positively

He developed positive thinking by repeating affirmations to himself on a regular basis and enlisting the support of his family and friends.

9. Focusing

Ben also kept focused on his goal by making sure that other projects did not take him away from his first priority.

10. Succeeding

Ben is due to move into his new house next year. There is much to be done, but he has an expectation of success and is already planning the celebration party. So you can see from Ben's example that it is possible to set goals and achieve them. The process need not be too demanding, and having the desire, belief, and expectation that the goal will succeed, he will ensure that he becomes one of the 90 percent of people who achieve their goals.

Section 4 will guide you through the goal-setting process to ensure that you give yourself the best chance of success in achieving your changes and projects.

STAGE 4
IDENTIFYING AND PLANNING FIRST STEPS

The primary function of the goal-setting process is to help you create a vision of how you want a particular situation to look like in the future. Rather than making a detailed action plan that sets out how to achieve your goal, as in the traditional method of goal-setting, developing one or two first steps toward your goal can be a more encouraging way of completing your projects. Seeing the achievement of your goal as a series of steps makes it a much more manageable process and easier to break down into bite-size pieces.

THE FIRST STEPS

Imagine that you are a new manager. Your goal is to learn to manage staff effectively and develop some basic management skills. The first step might be to identify the key management skills that you need to develop in order to fulfill your role as a first-time manager and to analyze your strengths and weaknesses against these skills.

It can be quite easy to identify and plan a first step but sometimes difficult to carry it out, so you may need help from others. For example, in the above situation, you may need to ask colleagues for their feedback to help you identify your strengths and weaknesses, or you might need to consult more experienced managers. You may need to draw on your Resource Pack of skills in Section 2, such as using assertiveness, to ask for feedback.

USING YOUR DOMAIN MAP

Return to your domain map and draw a fourth concentric circle around the outside. Record your first steps in the relevant sections.

STAGE 5
REVIEWING YOUR GOALS AND FIRST STEPS

When you have implemented your first step, it is important to review it.

THE LEARNING CYCLE

The review process has four stages:

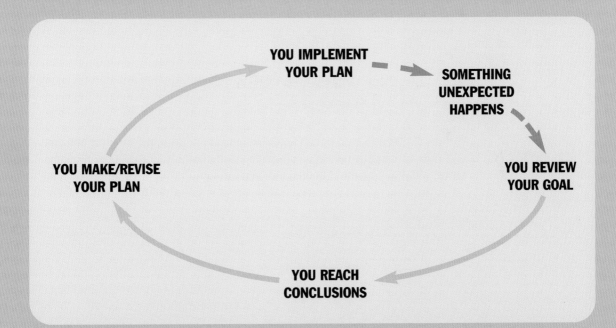

This model assumes that learning is a continuous process and that, to learn effectively, we need to complete the cycle. You can use the model to review your first steps and goals when the unexpected happens or when you have completed your first step. It can also be used for periodically reviewing your goals.

Case study

Reviewing your goals

At one stage during his project, Ben planned to sell his house and buy a less expensive house near the city. The plan was to rent the house out for most of the year, except between September and November, when he planned to return to the city each year.

1. Ben sold his house and purchased another property as planned (**implementing his plan**).

2. Then something unexpected happened. The stock market decline reduced the value of his pension fund and he needed to think again about the luxury of retaining a house in the city (**reviewing his goal**).

3. He sought expert advice from the bank and his financial adviser (**reaching conclusions**).

4. He decided to sell the property and invest the profit to supplement his pension (**revising his plan**).

By taking time out to review his goal in the light of an unexpected event, he was able to make a further decision in relation to his project that brought about an improvement in his financial situation.

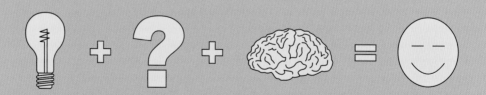

REVIEWING YOUR FIRST STEPS

This involves going through a similar process of review. Taking the example of the new manager again (see page 102), when you have analyzed your strengths and weaknesses, you will need to decide what you will do next to meet your development needs. You might opt to attend a management training course, and after completing the course, undertake a review of how the course helped you move toward your overall goal.

Step 1

You review the course and identify what you have learned. You monitor your performance over a month and identify where you have improved your management skills and confidence and where you still need help.

Step 2

You reach conclusions; perhaps you need more help in a particular area.

Step 3

You plan your next step. How might you get further help? Do you need more formal training or would finding a mentor be a more appropriate course of action?

Step 4

You implement the plan by taking the next step, with help where necessary.

Thus, the process of review can help you evaluate and set further steps in place. Develop the self-discipline to review your first steps at regular intervals and to review your goals when something happens that might affect them.

STAGE 6
EVALUATING OTHER COURSES OF ACTION

When you have identified and implemented your first step, you will often find that your next step involves examining different possibilities and courses of action. This will involve weighing the pros and cons for each of your possible choices and identifying your preferred option.

WEIGHING THE PROS AND CONS

Here is a method that will enable you to weigh the pros and cons of each course of action. You simply draw the diagram on page 107 in your Personal Portfolio and complete it for each possible course of action. It is a simple process that is effective in that it helps you be objective about making choices.

The example of the new manager and the different options available for addressing development needs illustrates how you might use this method for your own projects.

Don't neglect your feelings.

Option 1: **TRAINING COURSE**	**PROS:** • Meet other people • Quick • Good practice • Company will pay	**CONS:** • Terrified of looking stupid in a group • General—not specific to job	**CONCLUSION:** Not now
Option 2: **ONLINE COURSE**	**PROS:** • Flexible • Do it on my own time, at my pace • Easy to understand	**CONS:** • Boring • Not good for skills practice	**CONCLUSION:** Only as a supplement to other methods
Option 3: **MENTORING**	**PROS:** • One-on-one • Job-specific • Personally tailored • Confidential	**CONS:** • Only me and mentor • Not as good for learning skills	**CONCLUSION:** Consider as an option

THINKING AND FEELING

Use your thinking ability to identify the pros and cons, but don't neglect your feelings. In the example of the new manager, you might think that one of the ways to meet your training and development needs would be to attend a management training course. There might be a list of pros in favor of this course of action, such as meeting and sharing experiences with other managers who are in similar situations.

But what if you had a fear of being in a group with other people? This would mean listening to your feelings and identifying your fear as a con, which you would need to overcome if you were to attend a training course with other managers. Your feelings have, in this case, given you an insight into a possible barrier to achieving one of your options.

By analyzing your pros and cons at a thinking and feeling level, you can gain better insights into what choices to make.

STAGE 7
REMOVING BARRIERS TO SUCCESS

One of the main things that can hinder us from achieving our goals and completing our projects is failing to identify and remove the barriers that appear from time to time.

SELECTING OPTIONS

In the example of the new manager, one of the cons that was identified for the management training course option was a fear of being with a group of people. One way of dealing with this con would be to select another option, such as reading a management text-book. However, apart from this particular con, the training course would have been one of your preferred options.

An alternative course of action, therefore, would be to deal with your fear of being in a group by using some of the skills from your Resource Pack (see Section 2), such as challenging your negative inner voice or using some of the initiating strategies in the assertiveness skill (see page 46).

FORCE-FIELD ANALYSIS

The fact is that when you are making changes, for every positive step you take toward the change, an equal and opposite negative force will come to meet it. To progress, it is essential to move the negative forces out of the way. This can be achieved through a method called "force-field analysis," where the positive and negative forces are examined and strategies are developed in order to remove the negative forces and build on the positive ones. The process of force-field analysis can be used at the beginning of a project, when setting your goals, as well as during the project when you encounter difficulties.

Case study

Pat was thinking of a career change (see page 7). At the beginning of her project, she analyzed the positive and negative forces that existed in relation to her goal, which she set in the present, as if she had already achieved it. Similarly, Pat used the force-field analysis technique as if she was looking back in time, imagining that she had identified and removed the barriers that existed in relation to her goal. By writing them down as if she had already succeeded in removing them, she felt more confident and motivated to develop strategies to deal with them in the present. Her method is set out below.

Pat's goal was: "It is 2004 and I am working as a freelance management development consultant with a variety of clients who provide me with regular work." First, Pat identified all the positive and negative forces that were present in relation to her goal. Some of these are highlighted in the diagram below:

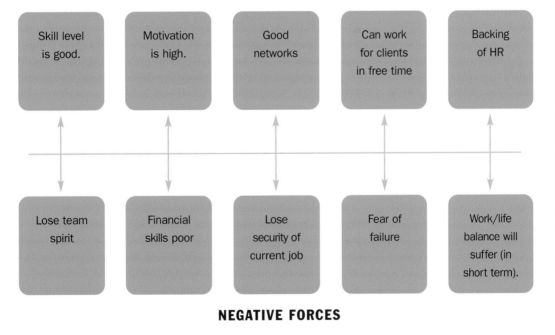

POSITIVE FORCES

Skill level is good.	Motivation is high.	Good networks	Can work for clients in free time	Backing of HR

Lose team spirit	Financial skills poor	Lose security of current job	Fear of failure	Work/life balance will suffer (in short term).

NEGATIVE FORCES

The next thing that Pat did was to make a list of steps to remove or get around the barriers, using some of the positive forces and the skills from her Resource Pack (see Section 2), and looking back as if she had already achieved the steps.

"To remove the barriers facing me, I have . . .

built up my network of fellow freelance consultants and arranged to meet them at regular intervals."

attended a financial management seminar and found a good accountant and financial adviser."

negotiated a clause in my severance package so that I can return to my previous organization within two years."

assumed I would succeed and found myself a mentor to help me think through difficult situations and provide me with support."

given myself three years to build my new business and developed the willpower to set aside time for myself and my family by writing it into my diary at the start of each year."

By writing down the list of steps, Pat developed a mini action plan, and because in her mind she had already completed it, she found it relatively easy to implement.

Action Plan

1.

2.

3.

4.

MAKING THINGS HAPPEN

If you don't remove the barriers to success, they will get in the way of your changes and result in you feeling defeated or lacking in motivation. In developing your strategies to remove your barriers, it is important to put your energy into things over which you have control and delegate or forget about the things over which you have little or no control. Then you will be able to make things happen without further barriers getting in your way.

For example, if Pat had tried to undertake all of the financial management of her new business without the support of expert help, she would have been setting herself a task that was overambitious and not fully within her control. She lacked the accounting and financial skills to ensure that the financial management of her business flowed smoothly. She therefore did the minimum that was necessary to introduce herself to the things she needed to know about financial matters and delegated the rest.

Notice how Pat also drew on her skills Resource Pack in developing and implementing the key steps to remove the barriers that were in danger of sabotaging her goal.

To progress, move negative forces out of the way.

STAGE 8
KNOWING WHEN YOU HAVE REACHED YOUR GOAL

It is important that you have ways of measuring when you have completed your projects and achieved your goals. Many experts recommend that with any project, you should identify some key "success criteria" that can be measured and can provide an indicator that the project has been completed or the goal has been reached.

DEVELOPING SUCCESS CRITERIA

There are several ways of developing success criteria. The first method (below) uses the technique of visualization to evaluate whether or not you have reached your goals, but there is an alternative for those who are uncomfortable with visualization.

VISUALIZATION EXERCISE

This will help you visualize what your project or goal will look like when you have achieved it. It uses your creativity to assist you in developing a clear picture of what success is like.

1. Get yourself into a relaxed position by doing a short relaxation exercise (see page 136).
2. Keep your eyes closed and imagine that you have achieved your goal.
   Begin to create a clear mental picture of:
   What it feels like: *Do you feel excited, elated, empowered, happy, and so on?*
   What it looks like: *What pictures do you see in your mind?*
   Whether there are any sounds you associate with it: *What can you hear?*
   Whether there are any tactile elements present: *What can you touch?*
3. Stay relaxed as long as you want, until you develop a clear sensory picture of your goal or project.
4. When you open your eyes, make a note in your Personal Portfolio of any images that you want to record. These will represent your success criteria.

AN ALTERNATIVE APPROACH

If you prefer to use a more tangible and logical method of developing success criteria, you will need to revisit your goal, written in the present tense. You can then ask yourself the following question: "Now that I have achieved my goal, what are the key criteria that inform me that I have been successful in reaching my goal?"

Here are the answers for some of the examples given in this book.

Ben would have some tangible success criteria, including a house in a part of the country that he wants to live in, a lifestyle that enables him to dine out once a week, and more choice to live the lifestyle he wants following his retirement.

Pat would also have some tangibles, including a database of clients, an office, and a network of associates.

Jane would have a redesigned room that meets her needs.

Even with this method, however, it is useful to bring in some sensory data, such as:

How do **Pat** and **Ben** feel when they have achieved success in implementing their changes?

What can **Jane** see, smell, and touch when her project is complete?

Whichever method you use, identifying success criteria is a very important part of getting things done.

If you don't have a feel for what success will be like, how will you know when you have achieved it?

STAGE 9
AVOIDING "CHANGE-BACK" MESSAGES

Many of us, when we make changes, affect other people with the changes that we make. Not everybody likes these changes, particularly if they have not been involved in developing the project from the beginning.

Case study

Ben had his retirement plan in place some years before he met Ellie, his wife. It was important for him to involve Ellie in his project as soon as they met, because the move to another part of the country would have a big impact on her life and work.

At first, Ellie was very unhappy about the proposed move. However, when Ben involved her in his plans from the beginning by using some of the skills in his Resource Pack, she gradually adopted Ben's goal. Ben was always prepared to compromise. If the particular part of the country he wanted to move to did not suit Ellie, he was happy to look at other options.

Ben did not receive too many "change-back" messages that would have diverted him from his lifelong goal, but this is not always the case.

STAYING ON COURSE

Imagine that you have always behaved in a passive way in dealing with your boss. One example of this is that you have always said yes when he requests that you work late. You then decide to make a change and begin to say no when asked to put in extra time. You do this in an assertive way, building in a compromise in that you agree to work late if the issue is important and urgent, but not as a general rule.

Suddenly, your boss sees a change of behavior, which may not meet his needs, and he might try various tactics to get you to change back to the way you behaved before you started to say no to his requests. For example, he might accuse you of being uncooperative or difficult, or threaten you in some other way to try to get you to change back to your old behavior.

You then have a couple of choices:

- **Change back to the way things were before.**
- **Stick with the change, since you know it is a reasonable thing to do and you feel perfectly within your rights.**

The second course of action takes courage, but if you stick with your resolve, the other person will eventually have to make a choice for himself about whether to continue to put pressure on you to change back or to accept the change and adapt his behavior in line with your new approach. Research has shown that often the other person will adapt if the change you have made is reasonable and you stick with your resolve.

Strategies

Here are some strategies for avoiding the risk of changing back.

✓ Revisit your goal and remind yourself why you made the change in the first place.
✓ Weigh the pros and cons of the two options—changing back and sticking to your resolve.
✓ Use your assertive skills to influence and persuade the other person.
✓ Involve the other person in your project so that he develops a sense of ownership and is less likely to ask you to change back.
✓ Practice developing your willpower.
✓ Identify the benefits for the other person of the change you are making.

Remember that by sticking with your goals and carrying your projects through to the end, you are likely to succeed in achieving your overall aims. Remember, however, the change equation (see page 8) and the need to assess the costs. If the cost of any change is too high, then **adapt, postpone,** or **reconsider** your goals.

STAGE 10
LEARNING FROM FAILURE AND CELEBRATING SUCCESS

Things rarely go perfectly, and you will experience both failure and success in achieving your goals. Both these extremes can be used to your advantage.

SURVIVING AND LEARNING FROM FAILURE

In Stage 5, the learning cycle helped you review your first steps and goals. This model can also be used to identify the things that have gone less well and that you would consider to be failures. No one likes to fail, but when you ask people what they have learned from most in their lives, it is the failures that have taught them the valuable lessons that build up their wisdom and insights.

The process of review is important here. Use the method of reviewing success in Section 1 (see page 14) and the learning cycle (see page 103) to assist you in reviewing your failures. Here are some things you can do to make failure less painful.

Be proactive. Use the learning review process to write down the key learning points, and promise yourself to change the way you do things. Ask yourself, "What will I do differently next time?" Make a note of your insights in your Personal Portfolio.

Celebrate it. Failure does not need to be the end of the world. Treat yourself to something you enjoy doing or allow yourself an indulgence.

Don't be embarrassed. Try to let go of the shame or humiliation you might feel as a result of failing—we all fail sometimes.

Share your feelings. Talk about your failure to a friend. This helps to get things off your chest and develop a sense of perspective.

Learn to laugh at yourself. Is there anything that you find even slightly funny or amusing about your failure?

Learn to forgive yourself. We all make mistakes and there is always another day.

CELEBRATING SUCCESS

Remember to reward yourself for your successes. Many of us complete one project and then move on to the next without taking the time to catch our breath. We can also fall into the trap of underplaying our success by putting it down to good luck or by minimizing the skills and effort that we put into achieving our goals.

In the same way that we can use the learning review process to review our failures, we can also use it to review our successes. Review your projects following their completion and draw out the things that went well and not so well. Celebrating success includes:

- Acknowledging the skills that helped you achieve your goals.
- Recognizing the input and energy that brought about your success.
- Daring to boast a little about how skillful, talented, and focused you have been in achieving your goals.
- Organizing a celebration to share with friends and family so that they can also join in your success.
- Treating yourself to something special, just for you—putting yourself first.
- Accepting compliments from others who acknowledge and congratulate you on your success.

Many of us find the process of celebrating success difficult. Build it into your willpower exercises by giving yourself a treat when you have completed a difficult stage of your project. Make celebrating even your minor successes a habit.

Allowing yourself to handle your failures well and celebrate success will provide you with the learning, enthusiasm, and motivation to achieve success in all that you undertake in the future. Don't skip this extremely important part of the process—you deserve it! Now turn to Section 4 to learn how to plan and implement your own projects.

Not everyone is perfect! If you don't succeed, don't give up!

Section 4

Practical Exercises

This section guides you through some simple exercises relating to your chosen project in order to assist you with its implementation and to check your understanding of the concepts described in this book. Use your Personal Portfolio to make notes as you go through the exercises. Everything you need to know to ensure you succeed in the projects that you undertake has been covered.

Now is the time to take a leap and say to yourself, **"Just do it!"**

EXERCISE 1
IDENTIFYING AREAS OF DISSATISFACTION AND CREATING A DOMAIN MAP

Use the change equation to identify your areas of dissatisfaction:

Change = dissatisfaction + vision + first steps > cost involved

Think of the different aspects of your life and make a note of the areas or relationships that you are currently dissatisfied with.

Dissatisfaction:

Dissatisfaction:

Dissatisfaction:

Dissatisfaction:

Make a domain map representing your key areas of dissatisfaction. Draw a circle that represents you, and then draw the first three concentric circles of your domain map, highlighting:

- those areas of dissatisfaction where you want to make changes (first concentric circle);
- a description of the current situation (second concentric circle), i.e., what it is like right now;
- your vision for the future, i.e., writing a statement of how you would like the situation to be (third concentric circle).

EXERCISE 2
IDENTIFYING PRIORITIES FOR CHANGE

TURN YOUR VISION INTO A CHALLENGE

This exercise helps you to translate what you would like to achieve from the statement of your vision in the third circle of your domain map into an action-oriented statement.

Turn your dreams and visions into challenges by rephrasing them as indicated below.

I will . . .

I will . . .

I will . . .

I will . . .

ASSESS YOUR WILL TO CHANGE

Make sure that you have the will to undertake your challenges. How much do you really want to change the areas of your life and work with which you are dissatisfied? Take each challenge one by one and ask yourself these questions:

- What are the payoffs or short-term gains for me if I stay with things as they are right now?
- What are the long-term negative consequences if I don't make the changes I want to make?
- What will be the benefits of change?
- Are there any negative effects of change that I will need to manage when change happens?

PRIORITIZE YOUR CHALLENGES TO SELECT YOUR FIRST PROJECT

Use these prioritizing criteria to help you to select your first project:

- How important is it—will there be serious consequences if I don't do it soon?
- Will it show some results very soon—is this a motivational quick-fix project?
- Is it the hardest project to deal with—do I want to do it first and get my most difficult challenge out of the way?
- Is it key to some of the other domains—does it need to be undertaken first because until this change is made, I can't move forward on the others?
- How much do I really want to make this happen?

EXERCISE 3
SETTING GOALS

Translate your challenge into a clear goal using the future mapping exercise in Section 3 (see page 94). Remember to write your goal down as if you have already achieved it.

There may be more than one goal or your goal may be broken down into several subsidiary goals. Develop a separate goal statement for each goal and subsidiary goal. Remember to include a date in your goal statement so that you have a schedule to work with.

It is (date) and I am . . .

It is (date) and I am . . .

It is (date) and I am . . .

It is (date) and I am . . .

Gather any other material that you want to keep with your goals, such as articles or photographs. Tell people about your goals and begin to involve the key people who will be affected by your goals.

EXERCISE 4
IDENTIFYING SUCCESS CRITERIA

Use either of the methods described in Section 3 (see page 116) to identify your key success criteria. These will give you a way of measuring the outcomes when you have achieved your goals.

My key success criteria are:

1.

2.

3.

4.

EXERCISE 5
REMOVING BARRIERS TO SUCCESS

 Using the force-field analysis described in Section 3 (see page 108), write down your goal and identify all the positive and negative forces that exist in relation to it. Plot them on a diagram, like the one below, in your Personal Portfolio.

My goal is:

POSITIVE FORCES

NEGATIVE FORCES

Next, keeping your thinking in the past, write down all the things that you have done to build on the positive forces and remove the negative ones.

To remove the barriers that faced me in achieving my goal, I have:

1. _____
2. _____
3. _____
4. _____
5. _____

EXERCISE 6
IDENTIFYING KEY STAKEHOLDERS

Undertake a stakeholder analysis (see page 52) for the project or change that you are tackling. Make sure that you don't forget anyone, and select one or two key people who you think it will be particularly important to influence within your project. It is also useful at this stage of the project to identify the people who will assist you or to whom you might delegate.

My key stakeholders are:

1. _____
2. _____
3. _____
4. _____
5. _____

The people that it will be most important to influence if I am going to succeed with this project are:

1.
2.
3.
4.
5.

The people that I will need help from on the project are:

1.
2.
3.
4.
5.

The people to whom I could delegate some of my tasks during the project are:

1.
2.
3.
4.
5.

EXERCISE 7
IDENTIFYING FIRST STEPS

Remember that seeing the achievement of your goal as a series of steps makes it a much more manageable process and easier to break down into bite-size pieces. Develop one or two first steps for your goal and include any steps that you have already identified to remove any barriers that will prevent you from achieving your goal.

The first thing I will need to do to achieve my goal is:

1.

Other first steps are:

2.

3.

4.

5.

EXERCISE 8
EVALUATING OTHER COURSES OF ACTION

For each of the first steps identified in Exercise 7, use the pros and cons method (see page 106) to identify the way forward for those that have generated several possible choices.

Option 1:	Pros:	Cons:	Conclusion:
Option 2:	Pros:	Cons:	Conclusion:
Option 3:	Pros:	Cons:	Conclusion:

My preferred way forward is to:

EXERCISE 9
PLANNING THE PROJECT

Develop a project plan using your diary to assist you in planning how you will allocate your time.

To consolidate your time, schedule sensible blocks into your plan according to the nature of the task.

If feasible, try scheduling certain tasks on particular days of the week and set aside parts of other days for working on major tasks. Alternatively, schedule different activities into the day according to your own best working pattern.

Work on the most important part of your project when your energy levels are at their highest—your prime time. Identify how long you can concentrate on one thing at any one time—this varies from person to person.

Use your diary to:

plan each year first

       plan each month next

plan each week

      plan each day at the outset

EXERCISE 10
REVIEWING GOALS AND FIRST STEPS

Build regular review periods into your project plan for your goals and first steps. It is also useful to use the review process (see page 103) when something unexpected happens that might interfere with the smooth running of the project or the achievement of your goals.

Remember to focus on successes as well as problems. Things sometimes occur that can assist with your goal or project and these are as important to review as the barriers.

Ask yourself these questions:

"What is going well in relation to my goal?"

"What is not going so well in relation to my goal?"

"What has happened that might hinder the achievement of my goal?"

"What has happened that might help with the achievement of my goal?"

"What adjustments do I need to make to my plan in the light of the answers to the above questions?"

"Is there anything else I need to do to keep my project on track?"

"Do I need to seek help, and if so, who might assist me?"

"When do I need to review my goals again?"

EXERCISE 11
INFLUENCING KEY STAKEHOLDERS

You will need to influence your key stakeholders and others who might become involved in your project. Use the following method to make you more successful in influencing those people.

Work through the influencing checklist in Section 2 (see page 53) to help you plan your conversations. Remind yourself of the five assertive skills (see page 55), and then find a friend with whom to practice your conversations. Ask for their feedback and use the lists below to check that your behavior is assertive, rather than aggressive, passive, or manipulative.

When I'm being **assertive**:
- I say what I want clearly and concisely.
- I make decisions for myself.
- I don't get put down.
- I stand up for my rights without violating those of others.
- I treat myself and others with complete respect and equality.
- I realize I am responsible for my own actions and feelings.
- I apologize when I have genuine regret.
- I am tough and stick to my plan when appropriate.
- I express my opinions, needs, and wants and listen carefully to other people's opinions.
- I am calm, relaxed, and confident.
- I feel energetic, powerful, confident, and satisfied.
- I expect win–win in disagreements.

When I'm being **passive**:

- I don't say what I want.
- I go along with other people's decisions.
- I allow others to bully, coerce, and ridicule me.
- I deny my rights and allow them to be violated.
- I don't accept responsibility for what is happening to me.
- I apologize too much.
- I find it hard to clearly express opinions, needs, or wants.
- I often put myself down.
- I have difficulty making eye contact.
- I can be hesitant and nervous.
- I feel frustrated, powerless, unhappy, hurt, and anxious.
- I expect lose–win in disagreements.

When I'm being **aggressive**:

- I say what I want, often demandingly and at length.
- I make decisions for others.
- I bully, cajole, and coerce.
- I blame and attack.
- I violate other people's rights.
- I treat others with less respect.
- I take responsibility for others.
- I say "I'm sorry, but . . ." and attack.
- I express opinion as fact and don't listen to others.
- I can be dominating, sharp, and brusque.
- I feel energetic, angry, frustrated, and powerful.
- I look for "win–lose" in disagreements.

When I'm being **manipulative**:

- I am indirect and expect people to know what I want.
- I drop hints.
- I wheedle, flirt, falsely flatter, and sulk.
- I am sarcastic.
- I manipulate people by playing on their feelings—often guilt.
- I behave passively with aggressive intention.
- I feel frustrated, angry, and powerless.
- I often end up with lose–lose in disagreements.

EXERCISE 12
USING SKILLS

Regularly return to Section 2 to review the skills Resource Pack
that will help you to be successful in implementing your projects.
Be honest with yourself and ask others for feedback on your
strengths and weaknesses.

Ask yourself these questions:

"What key skills am I using well?"

"Are there any skills I could be using more?"

"Do I need to develop any further skills? If so, what skills do I need to develop?"

"How might I develop these skills?"

"Who could I ask to help me with this?"

EXERCISE 13
GETTING REGULAR EXERCISE

In Section 2, we looked at how important it is to manage your stress and maintain a healthy lifestyle (see page 84). When working on projects, however, it can be difficult to remember to make time for some of the things that we know keep us healthy. A common omission is exercise. We become absorbed in a project and then neglect to take the time to exercise.

Exercise can make an enormous difference to your energy levels and motivation. Even a small amount of exercise during a break can mean the difference between reapplying yourself to your work after a break and feeling demotivated, discouraged, and ready to give up.

CHANGING YOUR LIFESTYLE

The problem with exercise is that we often feel that we need to go out of our way to build it into our lives—for example, by paying a visit to the gym or arranging a game of tennis with a friend. However, the most effective way of getting more exercise is to build more activity into your daily routine. It is important to select an exercise routine that suits your lifestyle; otherwise you will find it difficult to motivate yourself to exercise. Find a friend to exercise with if you find it hard to motivate yourself.

BUILDING EXERCISE INTO YOUR ROUTINE

Here are a few things that you can do to build exercise into your daily routine with minimum effort. Make sure that you only exercise at a level with which you feel comfortable. Build exercise into your project plan—twenty minutes three times a week is a good starting point. Select one or more of the following options.

- **Increase your walking pace and go for a brisk walk every other day for ten to twenty minutes.**
- **Always walk if you have to go somewhere less than half a mile away.**
- **Use the stairs instead of the elevator.**
- **Attend an exercise class during your lunch break.**
- **Buy an exercise video to use at home at the beginning or end of the day.**
- **When you take a short break from your project, use the time to exercise instead of watching TV.**
- **Make exercise a habit.**

EXERCISE 14
PRACTICING RELAXATION FOR STRESS RELIEF

Relaxation is a way of managing stress in the short term; the following routine can be practiced when sitting in a chair. It only takes five minutes to complete and can help you relax at any time of the day when you find your stress levels increasing. It is particularly useful in the middle of the day as a pick-me-up or when you are taking a break from your project.

STEP 1

Find a quiet place where you can sit comfortably. Make sure you are free from interruptions. Make sure your arms and legs are not crossed, and get comfortable.

STEP 2

When you are comfortable, close your eyes and consciously relax all your muscles, starting at the top of your head, down through your forehead, mouth, jaw, neck, shoulders, and so on. Become conscious of each muscle group as you relax them. Relax right down to your toes. Try to get into each group of muscles and imagine that you are going deeper... and deeper... into a deep, relaxed state. Take your time.

STEP 3

While you are relaxing, start breathing in deeply through your nose and out through your mouth. Listen to your breathing and notice that, as you relax, your breathing becomes deeper . . . and deeper. Enjoy the luxury of relaxing while you listen to your breathing. Notice the length of the pauses as you breathe out and before you breathe in.

STEP 4

Continue to breathe deeply, maintaining all your muscle groups in a state of relaxation. As you do, begin to count backward from ten to one in the pauses. So, breathe out—ten, breathe in—nine, breathe out—eight, and so on. Repeat the exercise, counting from one to ten.

STEP 5

Remain seated for a few minutes in your chair, keeping all your muscles relaxed, and breathe calmly. When you are ready, open your eyes and slowly stand up.

EXERCISE 15
GIVING YOURSELF TREATS

Being able to treat yourself is a necessary part of keeping focused on your goals, and it ensures that you reward yourself during and after the completion of your project. Treats are a way of celebrating success. Setting high standards for yourself is important in achieving your projects, but rewarding yourself for meeting your standards is equally important.

Treats are the rewards or gifts that we give ourselves for achieving success or for cushioning the negative effects of failure. It is important to treat yourself both when things are going well and when things are tough.

Treats don't have to be big or expensive; they can be little things like watching your favorite movie, reading a chapter of an enjoyable book, or taking your dog for a long walk.

1. **Make a list of all the treats you enjoy.**
2. **Go to your project plan and block out periods of time for treating yourself.**
3. **Make this a habit.**

If you find it hard to think of treats, as some of us do, ask your friends and coworkers how they treat themselves and try out some of their ideas.

EXERCISE 16
EVALUATING SUCCESS

When your project is almost complete, it is important to evaluate your achievements against the success criteria that you set at the beginning of the project. To do this, you need to return to your goal and look back at your achievements. This will enable you to sign off some of the aspects of your project and set in place other actions to ensure that any outstanding tasks are completed.

STEP 1

Revisit your goal.

STEP 2

Choose appropriate headings under which to describe your success. These can include the success criteria that you identified at the beginning of the goal-setting process. Remember to choose the headings that are meaningful to you.

STEP 3

List your achievements under each heading. Remember that because you are behaving as if you have already achieved success, these notes will be written in the present or the immediate past tense.

- It is important to list as achievements those factors that may not yet be fully completed, as well as those you have successfully completed.
- Only include things you have been able to bring about directly, or at least influence considerably.
- Make your statements positive and specific and add in as much "evidence" information as you can to support your achievements.

STEP 4

Identify the key events that led up to your success. These may include:

- Broad headings such as "Qualifications"; e.g., "I was a business major in college."
- Each individual achievement; e.g., "I have successfully employed a carpenter to build the new closets in the dressing room."
- Sensory achievements; e.g., how you feel or what you see.

Add in specific dates, who else was involved, and more "evidence" information wherever possible.

STEP 5

If necessary, establish some more goals, with specific schedules, to clear up any outstanding actions that have yet to be completed.

EXERCISE 17
CELEBRATING SUCCESS

Allow yourself the luxury of celebration when your project is complete. Do this as soon as possible after you have achieved your goals. In choosing a celebration, put yourself first, think big, and luxuriate in your success. You deserve it!

If you really want something to happen, just do it!

A FINAL WORD

This book has introduced you to skills techniques and methods that, if applied to your projects and changes, will ensure that you achieve success. Putting the steps and skills described in the book into action involves hard work and dedication. It is important to choose the techniques that best suit your personality and methods of doing things, and it is important to remember that there is no right or wrong way of achieving your goals.

INDEX

goal visualization 112
goal-setting 21, 122–3
influencing stakeholders 131
personal journal 20
planning 129
priorities 121–2
reflection 18–19
relaxation 136–7
reviewing goals 130
skills review 133
stakeholder analysis 125–6
stress management 136–7
success criteria 123
treats 138
willpower 38, 121
expression, anger 69
external self-esteem 88–91

factors
achievement 140
causes of stress 83
motivation 36
failure
coping 25
delegation 81
fear 16, 24–6
learning 20, 116–17
faster working 76
fear 42–4
failure 16, 24–6
management 45
feelings see also fear
action evaluation 107
confrontation 66–7
failure 116
handling stress 84
fielding the response 55
first steps 102–5
change equation 8
identification, exercise 127
review, exercise 130
flexibility
goals 99
schedules 71
fogging technique 55
force-field analysis 108–9, 124
frustration management 68–9
future mapping 100

goals
importance 15, 21
reviewing 101, 103–4, 130
setting 98–101, 122–3
visualization 99, 100, 112
guidelines
delegation 81
goal-setting 100–1

identification
anger 68
first steps 102, 127
priorities 96–7, 121–2
skills 27–31
stakeholders 52, 125–6
success barriers 108–9
influence 28–30, 52–3, 131–2
initiative 46–51
inner voice 39–45
insulation, time use 74–5
internal self-esteem 88–9
inventory, skills 27–8
involving people 16, 100, 114,
125–6

journal 20

key skills see skills
knowledge
anger 69
project/change 71
stress 84

learning
cycle 103
from failure 20, 116–17
lifestyle 85, 134–5

management
anger and frustration 68–9
fear 45
stress 136–7
time 16, 32, 70–7
manipulative behavior 49, 55,
132
margin for error 71
meetings 53, 76
mental pictures 99, 100, 112

monthly planning 72
motivation 9, 22, 36
moving into a new house case
study 52

negative inner voice 39–45

organization, delegation 78

passive behavior 48, 132
past projects 19
perfectionists 24
personal portfolio 18
behavior patterns 31
courses of action 106–7
failures 26, 116
personal journal 20
procrastination 23
skills 27
strengths and weaknesses
33
success criteria 112
physical exercise 134–5
planning 70–3, 101
delegation 78
exercise 129
first steps 102
positive messages 40–1
positive qualities 27–8, 41
priorities
identifying 96–7, 121–2
importance 15, 16
tasks 32
time 70–7
procrastination 23, 74

reactions, failure 25–6
reasons
change 9
stress 83
recognizing anger 68
reflection, past projects 18–19
relaxation 136–7
repetition, assertive skill 55
resolution, conflict 60–4
resources, planning 71
responses, conflict 60–1
responsibility 14, 23, 79

Acknowledgments

Executive Editor: Trevor Davies
Editor: Jessica Cowie
Design Manager: Tokiko
   Morishima
Design: Martin Topping at 'ome
Illustrator: David Beswick at
   'ome
Production Controller: Manjit
   Sihra

The author

Ann Jackman is an independent management development consultant with a wide range of clients in both the public and private sectors. She runs her own company, AFJ Associates, in the U.K., and also works with a variety of international clients. She specializes in mentoring senior managers, team development, management development programs for executives and managers, and life and career planning.